Evelyn Cowan was born in the old Gorbals of Glasgow and lived there until she was eleven, with her widowed mother and ten brothers and sisters. She attended Abbotsford Primary School and Strathbungo High School. She often maintains that she educated herself in the Gorbals Library, at evening classes and the creative writing classes of Glasgow University's Extra-Mural Department.

Evelyn Cowan has also written a contemporary novel, *Portrait of Alice*, and has had numerous short stories broadcast by the BBC. In the course of her career she has published many articles in Scottish and Jewish papers and periodicals. She was President of the Glasgow Writers' Club from 1979 to 1983. Evelyn Cowan, who has three sons and eight grandchildren, still lives in her beloved Glasgow.

SPRING REMEMBERED

A SCOTTISH JEWISH CHILDHOOD

Evelyn Cowan

CORGI BOOKS

SPRING REMEMBERED
A CORGI BOOK 0 552 99416 2

Originally published in Great Britain by
Southside (Publishers) Ltd.

PRINTING HISTORY
Southside edition published 1974
Corgi edition published 1990

This book is set in 11/13 Imprint by
Falcon Typographic Art Ltd.

Corgi Books are published by Transworld Publishers Ltd., 61-63
Uxbridge Road, Ealing, London W5 5SA, in Australia by Transworld
Publishers (Australia) Pty. Ltd., 15-23 Helles Avenue, Moorebank, NSW
2170, and in New Zealand by Transworld Publishers (N.Z.) Ltd., Cnr.
Moselle and Waipareira Avenues, Henderson, Auckland.

Made and printed in Great Britain by
Cox & Wyman Ltd., Reading, Berkshire.

Dedicated to the memory
of my most unforgettable character
my beloved mother
MARY BANKS COWAN

*Believe me! Spring remembered is more green
than any spring on earth has ever been*

TOM WRIGHT

CONTENTS

JOURNEY INTO THE PAST

Sometime in every human life there are moments of despair: moments when you want to rush back through the past into the arms of your mother; moments when you would like to be a little girl again, as I was, eight years old, warm and contented by the family fireside. Your memories of childhood may live in the womblike security of other streets in other cities. The reality of my dreams of childhood days dwelt in a street of tall, stately Victorian tenements named Apsley Place in the Gorbals of Glasgow.

If you set out now to look for this avenue of tree-lined memories, you would not find it. For the destruction of the old Gorbals is complete. Gone are the little back yards where you played football. The close where you courted your first love is no more. In place of those cherished days lies heap after heap of rubble soon to rise again in multi-tiered heights of grey characterless modernity. The juggernaut of the demolishers' steel hammers desecrates a world which, like childhood itself, will never return.

Here in my beloved Glasgow, amidst whose changing pattern I often lose myself, the planners play happily in their waste grounds of stone. They marshal the streets into uniformity and parade the drab buses like a regiment up and down parallel lines. Yet despite this organized chaos, the River Clyde flows calmly along although the red trams clanging south and the yellow trams clattering north over its proud bridges are now nothing more than museum pieces.

One winter's evening before the demolition was completed, I strolled through the Gorbals, past my old Abbotsford School. I turned into Apsley Place. The wind whistled round the corners. Over there a broken bedroom wall was embarrassingly bare to the sky, its pink wallpaper flapped in the breeze. On one side freshly-made cavities in the ground gaped at me like dark translucent pools. On the other side, shells of half-grown buildings seemed to contain the aching emptiness of all adolescents.

The dampness and the cold penetrated my substantial middle-aged female body. I felt as dreich and gloomy as the November evening in which I walked. Yet sometimes I was skipping along in the wake of my eight-year-old shadow.

There are days when I must, inevitably, go forward. And there are days when I would go back to another time, another generation: back to the early years of my large family of sisters and brothers, while they were all alive, young, eager, and full of hope.

It was a world of poverty which, to me, was not misery, but rich and happy. Back to the year 1929, when teenage girls were flappers, wore short tight dresses, and cut their hair in Eton crops, when the juvenile delinquents of that era roamed the old Gorbals streets in gangs calling themselves the 'Billy Boys' and the 'Danny Boys'.

I climbed high, for the price of a sixpence, up to the Gods in the gallery of the old Coliseum picture house. There I sobbed, in childish abandon, into a rag-like handkerchief, while Al Jolson (dying son clasped to his bosom) sang:

> *Climb upon my knee son-neee boy.*
> *Though you're only three son-nee boy.*
> *There's no way of knowing,*
> *There's no way of showing,*
> *What you mean to me, son-neee boy . . .*

It was late that November evening. The workmen had all gone home. Their nightwatchman's red fire burned high in its brazier. I pulled the silk scarf round my head and ambled over. As I stared into the upward licking flames, I imagined Apsley Place as it was in happier times.

That winter evening slowly changed into late afternoon

10

as I journeyed into the past. The street was wide and clean. Mainly peopled, at this time of day, with children playing out after school. A little man in a dark uniform crisscrosses the road in front of me. He carries on his shoulder a long fiery stick to light the gas lamps. Armies of tall chimneys puff smoke into an overcast sky. The shadows grow darker, but memories of childhood fill my heart with growing light as I recall our family story.

In summer the sun was so hot that it melted the tar in the roads. Only cold weather, and cold people, seemed miserable to me. Death had not yet imposed any tragic limit on hope. Only fun and mischief really existed. Life must always seem like that in childhood.

My mother was an impecunious widow. Only it's quite wrong to use such a word on her behalf. She would not have understood it. For she was completely illiterate and would have described herself as just plain poor. Yet, despite her lack of the written word, she was a woman of high intelligence and indomitable spirit. She had something which no formal schooling can produce. She had an educated heart.

As a grown woman with a family of my own, I know now how many terrible days of secret doubts and fear she must have had. But all my sisters and brothers remember is the laughter and the happy times when we were young and secure.

One moment I was standing by the watchman's fire in my present form: the next, I was skipping along down Apsley Place, in my eight-year-old body. Halfway down the street I stopped at a close. A small metal number plate nailed to the closemouth revealed the number 33 white and flickering in the gaslight.

Looking up, I could see two of our old neighbours leaning, comfortably on cushions, out of their opposite first floor windows. Mrs Schulberg, sharp-nosed matriarch of a runny-nosed tribe, peered short-sightedly down at me.

11

'Who's 'at down there?' She sniffed, wiping her nose with the flat of her hand.

'It's that wee Cowan girl. Evelyn, the youngest,' replied Mrs Kaplan, a small stout benign-looking woman.

'Och, she's the one that plays football and runs with the boys when the polis chases them.'

'Yeh, a tomboy, that girl is.' Mrs Kaplan adjusted her big breasts and leaned over more comfortably. 'Poor Mary Cowan. I dunno why she didn' give up some of 'em younger children when the Welfare man came. That time her husband died. She woulda been better off with some of 'em in a orphanage.'

'Ach, I dunno,' sneered Mrs Schulberg. 'You wouldn' understand a mother's feelings.' (This was a constant jibe at Mrs Kaplan's childless state.) They settled themselves in for a long gossip, such as I had already been hearing all my young life. I can still hear it trailing on into the night air.

Lingering briefly below their voices, I noticed a group of girls playing peever on the pavement. I gazed with long affection on my once best friend, plump-faced Rosie Schulberg. She tied one end of a skipping-rope to the spiked railing of the garden near the close. The other end of the rope was gripped, rather wistfully, by a crippled girl called Fanny Steinschriber.

Further down the street, my twelve-year-old brother Jacky, nicknamed Jumbo, shouted to me in the interval of a rough crowded game of 'hunch-cuddy-hunch'. Beside him smiled his friend, a dark, good-looking boy who was extremely bow-legged.

Idling in the close nearby another neighbour's boy, Natie Hornstein, grinned at me. He was a long, pale, ginger-haired boy, whose face I can see to this day; and as I leaned against the brown sweaty wall of the close, I looked at him in fascination. I often wonder whether the permanent green snotter is still running in and out of his nostril.

Pushing past him, I began to climb a wide semi-circular

staircase. I peered up the spiral of the wooden banister and called – 'Coo-ee! O-oh-pen! Cooooo-eeeee!' My youthful eyes gazed up at an octagonal glass-domed skylight. Approaching the third storey, I knew I was nearly there. 'Cooo-eee! O-oh-pen!'

Towards the end of the top landing I faced a stout oak door with shining brass letter-box, door handle, name-plate, and bell-pull. There I stood in my full adult height, on the rough fibre door-mat, shrinking into my girlish eight-year-old body. And I felt happy and excited, for I knew I had come home.

One of my older sisters had opened the door while my voice was echoing up the stairs. This was our familiar signal. The lobby remained dark, as strict economy demanded all unused rooms must be. I turned right along a small passageway, entered the bright doorway, and leaned backwards against the closing door. My sad shy weary eyes roved round that wonderful kitchen in fond remembrance. There was an air of warmth and cleanliness, despite an odd untidy garment here and there. On my left stood a big black shining kitchen grate. The gas mantle puttered overhead. A pair of silk stockings hung dangerously drying on a string nearby.

The heaped coal fire roared cheerfully up the chimney. Facing me, I saw the darkened kitchen window. Below it the tap still dripped into the sink. I walked forward and veered round a little to my right. A bed recess came into view. The bed was occupied by my brother Walter, three years my senior, though smaller and thinner than me. He lay confined with one of his recurring winter coughs.

About a foot away from the bed stood a long scrubbed wooden table, surrounded by an assortment of chairs of all ages and sizes, its near end half-covered with cups and saucers for the evening meal, its far end almost hidden by small drifts of flour, strainers, sieves, and spoons – the remains of a day's baking.

Over all this reigned my mother wearing a spotted white

apron, her face flushed from the hot oven. Turning, she brushed the table and swivelled round to put a sticky bowl into the sink. How nice it was to see Ma again! I feasted my eyes on her. She looked quite young for her fifty odd years. Her brown hair fell in soft waves; her lovely white skin was a smooth and gentle inheritance from her farming ancestors in Lithuania.

Ma would be startled if she could see me now that my dark hair is largely streaked with grey. But when she looked up from the busy kitchen table, her kind understanding motherly eyes soaked into mine. I marched stockily forward, and I was only eight years old.

She waved the floury rolling pin at me in mock anger. I walked towards her, confident and smiling. I never had a thrashing in my life, being, as I was, the adored little sister of a family of eleven children, only six weeks old in my mother's arms when my father died.

'Where you been?' Ma threatened, the pink of her face a little redder now. 'You know you had to get the stuff for them plants.' I knew only too well from what I had been escaping. A faint jab of remorse came into my mind. Then my heart started beating rebelliously, against this most hated of all our household chores.

It was the collection of horse-manure from the street to feed my mother's plants. This duty was handed down as each child grew older and the job became more hateful. Finally it came to me that there were also certain drawbacks to being the adored youngest. There simply was no-one to whom I could hand on this horrible task.

'I'm not doing it.' I began to cry. Tears rolled down my chubby face. 'I'm not going away down there for everyone to laugh.' Ma's eyes lit up for battle. She could be quite soft in some matters. But as regards her plants and the care of all living things she set herself into pure granite.

'You are so, my gel,' she said threateningly. I could see by her face there was no way out. So I thought it over quickly.

14

I decided that the best time was early in the morning when no-one would see me.

'I'm cold and I'm feeling a bit sick,' I lied. 'Please, I promise I'll do it in the morning.' Ma's experienced eyes ran over me. I knew I would be lucky to get away with it. She had become, by necessity, an expert on children's ailments and was not at all deceived. There I stood, red-cheeked, sturdy, and healthy. Perhaps the thought of one sick child already in bed made her hesitate. She relented and I was temporarily reprieved.

'Now, mind you. First ting in the morning. You get that stuff before you go off to school' were her goodnight words to me.

I thought of Ma's plants while undressing by the roaring kitchen fire.

The plants were all over the house. There was one in the hall near the coat-stand, which we usually tripped over in the dark, because we were running away from the frightening shadows of its outstretched legs. Most of Ma's plants were aspidistras in large brass bowls mounted on tall mahogany stands which she picked up at second-hand furniture sales.

There were two or three in the 'big front room' facing the street. She even had one in her bedroom by the window. The only exception to the aspidistras was one solitary tomato plant. It stood on a narrow ledge just inside the kitchen window. That plant and its hardy stubbornness resembled my mother's struggle for survival.

The watery winter sun blinked down for a short time each morning, wedging its way into our kitchen between the towering back wall of Motherwell's grain mills and the tenements. My mother nursed the tomato plant each day like a baby.

It was not until years later, when Ma had a garden of her own, we realized she had 'green fingers'. Everything she planted responded to her loving care and grew up gratefully. The next morning, I awakened and rose very early. My small brain had planned it all during the troubled night. No-one could possibly be up so early. I would nip downstairs, shovel up the manure, and dash back home before even the milkman was about.

A faint glimmer of light seeped into our bedroom through some thin net curtain. I could see my sister Kate roll blissfully, in her sleep, into the warm groove I had just vacated.

In the next bed Ma lay snoring gently. Across the bedroom loomed a large white mountain which I knew to be my big brother George crushed into a bed far too small for him.

Shivering and hating the cold as always, I quietly dressed. I pulled on my old football jersey and tiptoed into the lobby. There lay a row of shining but worn shoes near the front door. This was one advantage of getting up early that I rarely gained. You could choose a pair of shoes which were not too shabby and which almost fitted you.

I trudged down the dim gaslit stairway. In one hand I held a shovel and in the other an old battered pail. I peered out of the close sideways through the garden railing. With my over-large jersey sleeve I pushed back the fringe of my hair and wiped my watery eyes. I could see there was no-one about. The coalman had just gone by with his horse and cart, shouting, 'Coal briquettes! Coal briquettes!' It seemed surprisingly early for him. I feared the noise of his cries would wake someone.

'*COAL BRI Q U E T T E S*!' . . . The coalman's breath shot out in the cold November morning like shafts of new steel from a furnace. The horse's bowels had been moving continuously. I ran out to the middle of the road, scooped up some steaming dung in my shovel, and deposited it quickly in my pail. Oh how glad I was that there was no-one about! This humiliating task nearly over, I rested the pail for a moment in the centre of the street. The shovel clattered noisily down in the quite street. Suddenly a first-floor window shot open and a girlish voice shouted, 'Hey, you! Does your ma not feed you?'

I might have known. It was my fat fair-weather friend Rosie Schulberg. Either I had mistaken the time, or the coalman's cries and the clattering of the shovel had awakened the immediate neighbourhood. Another window flew up. Out came the pale-green, red-topped face of Natie Hornstein. 'Hey, you, the wee one!' he screamed, 'what you got there?' And without waiting for an answer he gleefully exclaimed, '*We* get custard with *our* pudding!'

Natie threw back his head and laughed at this old joke – laughed, and sniffed his green snotter at the same time. This was quite a remarkable feat. By this time, windows were clicking up on all sides like camera lenses. I had grossly misjudged the time. For almost everyone of wakable age in the block was fully dressed and peering out at me.

Standing beside my steaming pail, small, angry, and forlorn, I glared up at all the gaping black squares of windows, shafts of light, and laughing false teeth. My eyes smarted with frosted tears. Quickly I tucked the shovel into the smelly contents of the pail, gripped the iron handles of both and ran with my head down, like the experienced footballer I was, to the safety of the close.

MY ODD LITTLE CALENDAR

In our ghetto-like existence, the city of Glasgow seemed far away, the world even more remote. The year 1929, notorious for its corroding international depression, made no difference to our family. We were poor anyway, as were the majority of our neighbours in the Gorbals. Generally they were tailors, cobblers, butchers, and small shopkeepers who had arrived in Scotland at the turn of the century on the run from pogroms or long military service in their native Russia, Poland, or Lithuania.

The men worked long hard hours in their shops. Their wives became prematurely old from constant childbirth and continuous monotonous domestic work. As for us children, the streets were our nursery. Games of football in the back green were strictly forbidden. We were usually on the run from the police.

At all times we were haunted by a tall policeman with a graveyard pallor whom we nicknamed 'Paleface'. Any night you could see him swinging round the corner of Apsley Place, as though his face were illuminated. He seemed determined to enforce the law against us hardened criminals. At the shout of 'COP!', half the children in the street disappeared through the closes, across the back yards, over the dykes, into lanes of escape.

We played our naïve little sex games in the darkness of the dunny at the back close. Their queer rites and rules seemed innocent enough to us. For the sight of a boy's semi-nude body aroused no curiosity in me, bathed as I was with my two brothers every Thursday night.

However, one incident which involved me did not have such innocent consequences. Six of my brothers' friends aged about twelve, offered me one ha'penny each to undress in the dunny and show them the lower half of my girlish torso. They were then to unbutton their trousers and reveal themselves to me.

I considered this a fair proposition. And the thing that appealed most to my eight-year-old mentality was the thought of all those bags of chocolate drops and aniseed balls I could buy at the wee sweetie shop with my six ha'pennies. Nobody was going to touch me, I thought, and I reckoned I would not see anything I had not already seen many times before.

I agreed to the rendezvous. We met at the iron-barred door of the cellar in the close. Someone lit a candle. We formed a circle and waited, seven little innocents not knowing how to proceed. Then my big brother Jumbo turned up only minutes before the orgy. He had got wind of the whole thing through an informer in the street. Jumbo punched up all the boys good and proper. He slapped my face and added a warning never to do such a thing again.

The consequence of this episode was that Jumbo had a blackmailing hold on me for a number of months. Any time he did not want to run an errand for our mother or to get himself a bottle of ginger pop, he knew where to find me and put the pressure on. If I refused, he laughingly threatened to tell Ma about my escapade. This was my first and only attempt to earn money from sex. My knowledge of the sex act was still nil. But I learned a lot about blackmail.

My father, Simon Cowan, a tailor by trade, had been a small dapper man, virile, irascible, and compulsively over-generous – a good reason why he never had any money. Also he was a man who could not settle down in one town for any length of time. To quote a well-known Yiddisher expression, he had no 'zeets-flaish'. In other words, he had 'ants in his pants'. As an end to all his loving good nature, his quick temper, his fears and his failings, he suffered from chronic asthma.

It was in one of his attacks that he died suffocating at

the untimely age of forty-six. During his lifetime he opened and closed, albeit rather hastily, at least a dozen men's outfitters' shops in various parts of the country. Perhaps it is true that an ill wind always blows some good. My mother, now widowed with eleven children, found poverty grinding. But for the first time in her married life she had a permanent home.

The welfare state did not arrive until some thirty years later. We were not cushioned by the benefits of today. My father had been a self-employed master tailor. Ma had no claim to any pension. We could, however, apply for money from the public assistance in the case of dire necessity; and so she did from time to time, although it was considered the last shame before the poor-house.

At the time of my father's death our fortunes were at their lowest ebb. The ages of the family ranged from the eldest girl of nineteen years down to myself at six weeks.

The differences in our ages was usually eighteen months. Except for three years between my brother Walter and me. Surely Papa must have been out of town for some time on one of the wild business schemes!

On his death every member of the family who was of working age, and some who were not legally so, went out into the City of Glasgow – job-hunting. But Lily, the third eldest of my sisters, hit on the idea of travelling into the outlying villages to sell drapery to the housewives. This was by no means an original idea. She had seen other people in the Gorbals carrying goods from small warehouses like Goldbergs in the Candleriggs. The travellers explained to her how they sold the garments round the doors of the townlets which dotted industrial Lanarkshire like measles on a child's swollen face.

Lily was just seventeen at the time of our father's death. She was a small, fair, plumpish girl, maybe not quite so pretty-pretty as some of my other sisters. Yet she had that indefinable quality of which J. M. Barrie once wrote: 'It's a sort of bloom on a woman. If you have it (charm) you don't need to have anything else; if you don't have it, it doesn't much matter what else you have.'

She had this charm. When Lily looked up at you, her tousled head held a little to one side, her blue eyes alive and (at that time) always laughing, she was quite irresistible. I loved to hear how it all began. They were my favourite round-the-fire evening stories. She told me she opened her battered suitcase one winter's day at the first house in Glenboig, a mining village.

'A shilling a week,' said Lily. 'Look, here's a really good pair of sheets, Missis, for only eight shillings and elevenpence a pair.'

The housewife edged the door a little wider to examine the linen. 'Your friend down the road has just taken two pair. She knows they're a real bargain. And only a shilling a week,' Lily repeated.

'Och, aa-right. I'll tak the two pair the same.' The miner's wife reached into a pocket of her printed cotton overall for her purse. 'Here's two shillin for ma deposit.' Lily withdrew a bundle of blue club cards from her case. On the covers my sisters had all helped to print by hand the grand title

Lily Cowan & Co., Drapers,
33 Apsley Place,
Glasgow, C. 5.

On the inside page of the little blue book she wrote in pencil: *'Mrs MacInulty, 10 Glenfield Avenue, Glenboig'.* Down below on the ruled line she scribbled:

2 pr Sheets at 8/11 each pair – 17/10
Less deposit – 2/–

15/10 balance.

21

'Thank you very much, Missis,' she said politely. 'I'll see you next Thursday. If it's not me myself it'll be my sister.'

The Cowan girls were now in business. All her gay beguiling ways did not detract from Lily's astute business ability. The system which she initiated by sending three or four sisters out into different towns looking for more and more customers was soon to be multiplied by sharp businessmen many times over. In later years this credit drapery trade became real big business. The packman, the wee society man, or the shilling-a-week woman was accepted in almost every working-class home as naturally as the days of the week on which they called.

In present-day Glasgow you will find their descendants: distinguished, grey-haired, steely-eyed tycoons working in city offices. On their desks stands a picture of their Papa, who started by knocking the doors and tramping the roads of the Scottish countryside.

There was one character in our street. Customers called her 'Jeanie the Jew'. She travelled all over the West of Scotland with a black waterproof pack on her back. She could neither read nor write. Yet she knew to a penny how much each customer owed her, what goods were purchased, how much added on to the account. Every little sum remained in her memory. Her integrity was much respected by everyone. She was never short of a meal, a hot cup of tea, or a wee chat at a warm fireside. This was the general pattern of friendly trade typical of that time. Both of Jeanie the Jew's sons distinguished themselves in the legal profession; and one of them later became a famous judge in the Court of Session in Edinburgh.

It would be nice to say at this point that our family subsequently became millionaires, and that you are about to read a real rags-to-riches story. But, truly, it was not so. We made a modest hard living from the first day in Glenboig right through my mother's lifetime.

The snow lay deep enough to bury you. The icy wind blew so sharp, it literally cut your face. My sisters were out, come hell or high water, collecting the money and delivering the goods.

This heroic fight against the elements was always a feature of our trade. It was not histrionics, but merely elementary economics. We were contained in the tight vicious circle in which all working people find themselves. Our customers needed to work to pay their rent, their coalman, their grocer, and also to pay us for their clothing. In turn we had to go out on our day's collection because we owed money to our wholesalers for the goods supplied. Starting with no capital, my sisters obtained extended credit from warehouses. Meaning that the drapery we bought was not payable for three months after purchase. By that time we had to have enough money to pay at least one bill each month. There was no missing a day's work.

When I was a little girl our family had a magic word. This word was 'appro'. I had no idea what it meant. The dictionary in school did not enlighten me. Yet, faster than the pantomime fairy's wand, appro conjured up all the new dresses that my seven sisters desired. Every party, every dance of the Gorbals social season was enhanced by the Cowan girls tricked out in the latest flapper gowns matched with tight cloche hats. Even the long beads and jangly bangles were artfully wizarded by appro.

One day I solved the mystery. Not by coincidence, there had been a big dance the previous night. I was sent with a large brown cardboard box over the Suspension Bridge, the pedestrian's life-line from the Gorbals to the city, to a wholesale store in town. Opening the printed note which I had to hand in with my bundle, I read: '*Please find returned herewith, 7 Dresses taken on approval*.'

My sister Lily was our driving force. She was the hardest worker, the brains behind our little organization. But very soon the mining areas were overrun with travelling credit

23

drapers. Times were hard. The miners' wives were grim, poor, work-worn, and hard to deal with.

Never one to give in, Lily came up with another idea. By this time she was twenty-five years old. The firm of Lily Cowan & Co., Drapers, would then be the same age as me, about eight years old. Lily had been married five years previously to a nice young Jewish tailor. Their happiness appeared to be marred only by its lack of children.

She lived in a small flat in the flourishing new suburb of Shawlands. In those days it was considered very high-class for any Jewish person to live outside the Gorbals. It cost a threepenny fare on the red tram back to the south side of Glasgow. This was a tremendous distance. Sometimes we needed sandwiches for such a journey.

Lily visited Ma and the kids almost every day. She had made herself responsible for my school clothing and also helped towards the upkeep of the younger children. This saved Ma, at last, from the indignity of the Public Assistance Board. Still young and gay was Lily, and the most generous, lovable, goodhearted person I have ever known.

She died comparatively young. Hers is a tragic tale. For me it was the end of childish dreams, the point of no return. I grew up the day she died. But that's not the story I'm telling now.

It was nearly four o'clock on the day of one of her visits. Off school for some trifling reason, I was playing by the fire with a little beaded bag which big sister Lily had just brought me – though I'd much rather have had a pair of football boots.

The fire licked hungrily up the black kitchen range. Ma, in command at the table, buttered thick slices of brown bread. For the children were due in from school and equally as hungry. 'What do *you* think, Ma?' Lily's soft voice (eyes to match) appealed to her.

'I think it's a good idea.' Ma wiped her hand across her apron, piled the bread high on a plate and started to pour out cups of milk. Lily tapped a pencil on a scribbled paper. She was always neatly dressed in tailored suits with a little frilly blouse edging through, her unruly curls set off by a small toque hat, her feet in trim court shoes.

'We could rent this house in Rothesay for the summer, Ma. I've been down to see the man, Mr Bone, and he'll let us have it for £30 for three months. We could do all our business from there. Things are very hard in Bellshill and Glenboig. There's been unemployment and a lot of bad debts. So I think we'll try the Clyde coast.'

'Sounds like a good ting to me.' Even after years in this country, Ma always had trouble pushing certain English words through her teeth. 'We get the business done. And the children get the fresh air and sunshine at the same time. Sounds goot.'

Lily nodded her head in agreement. 'And from Rothesay we can get a boat over to other seaside towns like Largs and Dunoon. There's lots of money going about when the local people rent their homes for the summer months. We can sell dresses and jumpers in the tearooms. The waitresses earn good money in the season.'

This concentration of the business in Rothesay was one of the reasons why my little classroom-made calendar read quite differently from those of all the other children in Abbotsford Public Primary School. Being Jews we did not celebrate Christmas. We had a festival of our own called Chanukah, when Ma lit a large coloured candle, and every night added another smaller one until on the last night we had eight small coloured candles burning together with the leader from the first night. We sang our Chanukah songs, which we often parodied with our own lyrics: in a mixture of Hebrew and Scots.

Maw ow soor
yi shoo aw see:

25

the cat's in the cupboard
and he needs a wee-wee.

We exchanged little gifts which were all home-made. It was a rare sight to see a Christmas tree, probably because there was only one non-Jewish family in our three-landing close. And in the whole of Apsley Place there was only a mere handful of Protestant and Catholic families.

Through the cold wintry gloom, the lights of Chanukah shone forth, illuminating our Jewish home with its message of hope and courage. Reminding us, yet again, of the faith, zeal, and moral fortitude of Judah Maccabee and his men.

So my calendar read 'Chanukah' instead of 'Christmas'. I knew it was winter. New Year is the Scottish national festival. To me, there was nothing like the thrill of a Guid New Year in Glasgow. Slowly crowds gathered at Glasgow Cross. At midnight, the huge bells of the Tolbooth pealed out a welcome to the New Year. Although Jewish people have their own New Year in September, we youngsters in the Gorbals celebrated the night of 31 December with equal delight. My odd little calendar contained New Year's Eve, twice over.

In the spring came Pesach, the festival of the Passover, when we ate only special unleavened bread. We ate no food which had flour as an ingredient. Every single cup, saucer, plate, spoon, fork, knife, pot, pan, and kitchen utensil had to be new, untouched, or brought out of storage from the last Passover.

On the eve of the Passover, Ma went round the house with a large candle and a feather. This was to brush away bread crumbs with the feather, then burn them out with the candle from every corner, so that anything connected with bread or chometz would be banished from our home.

My mother, though not fully understanding why she did all this, was a practising Jewess descended from strictly orthodox Lithuanian Jews. She carried out every religious

26

law, no matter at what personal sacrifices, financial or other-wise.

In many instances, preparing, cooking, and baking went on well into the wee small hours of the night. My calendar now read 'Pesach'. I knew it was springtime. Then on 31 May of every year out came the largest wicker hampers you have ever seen. Together with every battered trunk and case that could be borrowed round the neighbours.

For my mother, with her eleven children, some sons-in-law, three grandchildren, and several assorted fiancés, was about to spend her annual three months 'vacation' in Rothesay on the Island of Bute. This entailed three hours sailing by paddle steamer from Broomielaw quay at the Clydeside.

So my odd little calendar read, 'June, July, Rothesay'. My girlish heart sang, 'June, July, Rothesay'. I knew it was summer. Not until I was almost grown up, did I learn that Rothesay was not the month after July in the correct sequence of months of the year.

With the exception of Ma, we all returned from the island sunburnt and healthy. She had her usual kitchen pallor. Now it was only a matter of weeks before Rosh Hashannah, the Jewish New Year, in September. For us children, a sol-emn festival of prayer with tedious best clothes synagogue attendance.

Then, quick as a minute, the leaves blew down Apsley Place, autumn blended into winter again. It was Christmas, which we do not celebrate. We had our own festival of Chanukah, when Ma lit a small candle and . . . And so on, as I thought then, for ever and ever, Amen.

PASSOVER

I sat down at my first lesson in the Talmud Torah Hebrew school in the old Gorbals of Glasgow. *'B'raishees,'* the student Rabbi read out. *'B'raishees,'* my childish voice repeated. The youth intoned, *'B'raishees,* in the beginning, God created the heavens and the earth.'

And what a lovely solid earth it seemed to me, as I trotted down Abbotsford Place from my Sunday morning school. For it was springtime. Almost Passover time. Ma had all the mattresses airing out of the back windows. My sisters were turning out rooms and polishing brass plant-pots.

The whole of Apsley Place was emerging from its winter grime. From our third-storey front room window, I indulged in my Sunday morning hobby of staring down into the Schulbergs' front kitchen window. Mr Schulberg, in his nightshirt, gallantly helped his wife down from the kitchen recess bed. He was always most courteous to her in the morning.

Most of the children in the street already had their new clothes for the festival. Ma tried to put a good face on for everyone. But business was not so good. We had not fully embarked on the Rothesay venture. So Ma thought she would set herself up, in the meantime, as an agent for Passover groceries. It seemed like a nice quick profit for just a few weeks' work prior to the seven days of the Passover.

Even the regular grocers had to hire separate unused shops so that they could prove no food had touched bread, and that they were kosher for Passover.

Ma showed the Rabbi, who was in charge of such matters, the clean front room which she intended to use as a store. It had been thoroughly scrubbed from ceiling to floor. He saw no objection and granted permission. Ma then instructed one of my sisters to write to the firms of Rakusens and Bonns. They agreed to supply her. They were the only manufacturers of matzo (unleavened bread) and sundry Passover delicacies in the whole of Great Britain.

She gave a sigh of relief as I read to her their letter of acceptance. But she had to have a guarantee by a responsible person that all the bills would be paid. This proved no problem. For most of the people in the Gorbals of Glasgow had a rough, trusting respect for Mary, the hard-working widow woman.

About the beginning of April, huge cartons eight feet high began to arrive at Number 33 Apsley Place. The carrier's men were told to leave them in the well of the close. My two brothers, Jacky and Wally, and myself leaned over the wooden balustrade three flights up. For once in my young life, I had no fear of falling down, down, down. The big brown cartons waited with open tops to receive me. Where could I fall but into a soft safe haven of matzo meal puddings?

Ma yelled up at us. 'Hey, you keender. Come down at once and help wid the boxes!' Usually there was a repeat before any of us obeyed an order. This time we needed no further invitation. We slid down the banisters one after another until we reached the bottom. My mother, perched on top of an extra high ladder, delved into the cartons. She emerged from time to time with boxes of matzo. Her long hair piled in a bun, she now wore glasses and they kept sliding down her nose.

My sister Kate, a studious bespectacled girl, absent-mindedly ticked off the items from an invoice, at the same time glancing at her library book. Peering up at her, I read out slowly – '*Brave New World,* by Aldous Huxley'. I had already skimmed through it. I read everything I could lay my eyes on, always picking out the naughty sexy bits. They were so interesting, next to conversations, in books. The bits that

29

fascinated me most in that book were all about having babies on a conveyor-belt system.

Kate had taken me to the Gorbals Public Library, filled in an application, and got me a junior ticket. It was as though she had given me a ticket to heaven. The pleasures of *Little Women*, *The Scarlet Pimpernel*, *The Count of Monte Cristo*, *A Tale of Two Cities*, were awaiting me. Any person who introduced me to such a treasure-cave would have my undying gratitude. But on top of this, I simply adored my sister Kate. She was my childhood idol.

Kate had finished peering short-sightedly at the Passover invoices and started helping Ma to unload the boxes. They piled our arms with boxes. And we children climbed up to the big front room, where another sister, Annie, stacked them against the wall.

We ran up and down, arms full of matzo boxes, sometimes falling over ourselves, giggling and singing little songs which we learned in Chader (Hebrew School). All this attracted the attention of the other children in the close. It was not long before we had a small army of helpers like little pygmies, toiling and singing, toiling and singing, up and down the stairs of our tenement.

After all the goods were checked into the house, we children slept, while Ma and the girls worked through the night making up orders for delivery before the eve of the festival. Previously Ma had been around the adjacent streets (Abbotsford Place, South Portland Street, Oxford Street, Main Street, Cumberland Street) canvassing for orders.

The response was surprisingly good. She even had orders from far-away districts. One person recommended another. It was not that there was any shortage of Jewish grocers' shops in Main Street, Gorbals – quite the contrary. But everyone knew that my mother needed the shilling or two. And a lot of orders were given more in sympathy than in the normal course of commerce.

The delivery of Pesach groceries was great fun. My brothers and myself did this after school. Once we discovered there was a two-penny or threepenny tip to be made, there was no holding us back.

The most important part of the festival of Passover, which commemorates the escape of the Jews from Egypt in ancient times, takes place on the first two evenings. It is more or less a big family dinner party with certain religious rituals; and it celebrates the fact that although the Angel of Death killed the first born of all Egyptian families, including Pharaoh's son, he passed over the houses of the children of Israel and spared them. These two evenings are called 'Sader' nights.

One late afternoon on the eve of the first Sader, Ma came to Wally and me. 'Here, you two! Here's a order that got left. Would you know how to get to Pollokshields? You turn right at Eglinton Toll.'

Wally, a thin delicate boy, seemed a bit afraid of the distance. 'What if we get lost, Ma?' Wally sniffled. She flicked him with a wet dish-towel. 'Ask someone. You gotta good Scotch tongue in your head. Have you?'

With this, Wally and I picked up the brown box and, one at each end, set off for Eglinton Toll. The tie-on label read: 'Mrs A. Goldfarb, 10 Bruce Road, Pollokshields, Glasgow, South 1.' We trudged along for about an hour, resting a while from time to time. It was getting dark. The streets gradually became wider. Houses loomed larger. Distances from the street, up the drive, to some of the stately homes seemed greater than the whole of Apsley Place. Gas-lit lamp-posts cast dark fingers on the pavement.

There was not a soul to be seen. Only our two little figures: a thin boy and plump little girl, gripping their precious box and peering into the darkness. 'What do you think, Wally? There's no-one to ask.' I began to cry. 'Are we lost? We'll never get home.'

Wally squared his small shoulders. He was always calm in a crisis. 'Now, don't worry. I'll get you there and I'll

31

get you back.' With Jacky always towering over him, it was not often he got a chance to be big brother to me. We leaned against the spiked railing of a garden. Some branches from a drooping tree blew over and touched Wally's neck. He jumped. We quickly glanced around us. There was no-one.

'If only we could see someone to ask the way. Here! Doesn't that sound like something?'

There was a crunch like footsteps on gravel. Out of the shadows of a lamp appeared a black figure. I screamed. I started to run. Wally grabbed me. I turned around. It came nearer. We saw a gleam of silver buttons. It was the large arm of the law. I shouted '*COP!*' from habit and made to run off again. The policeman barred my way. Wally gripped my hand. 'Don't run away. They're not all like Paleface. Maybe he'll help us.'

'Och, yes,' said the policeman in a kindly Highland accent. 'And what have we got here?'

'It's me and my wee sister.' Wally looked up at him.

'And fwhat are you tooing inteed around these parts?' the cop enquired.

'Please, we're delivering for my mother's grocery business. We're looking for a place called Bruce Road,' said Wally respectfully.

'Och, man, that's not far from here.' The policeman lifted my end of the cardboard box. 'Come along now, boys and girls. And I'll take you there.'

He took a left turn, then another, up a wide avenue. 'There you are now, mi children. Here is Number Ten.'

'Oh, thank you very much.' We were not too sure whether to call him 'sir'. We had never been so close to a policeman before. Our running distance was usually about two hundred yards from them.

'That's aa-right. Take two turns, remember now, and another one to the left. And you will be back tae the road leading to the south side of the city.'

'Thanks a lot.' We waved as he made off. Carrying our box, we tramped up the long drive.

Huge pillars stood at each side of the door. We rang the bell, tired and weary, glad to shed our load for a minute. A small jovial man in white shirt and braces opened the door.

'Oh, yes,' he laughed. 'What's this?'

'It's the Pesach order, please, sir,' said Wally.

'Well, my goodness! It's just as well I'm not waiting for it. It's nearly Pesach now.'

Our hearts sank again. We were going to be late for our own Passover at home. 'Never mind. Come in a minute. I know your mother well. Tell her everything was all right.' He beckoned to two dark handsome youths, who were hovering in the background.

'Here, boys, take this box through to the kitchen.' His two sons removed the grocery box. We stepped inside the warm hall and gasped in wonder. We had never before seen a carpeted room or, for that matter, one with crystal chandeliers. Mr Goldfarb's voice brought our gaping eyes back to him. 'Here you are, then, children. Try and be quick getting home.' He pressed a shilling into each of our hands. We were overwhelmed with this sudden fortune. A shilling!

Hand in hand, Wally and I danced away through the dark streets, impervious now to their menacing shadows. We were rich. We were rich. Yes, rich, and I knew what I would do with the money. I would buy Ma a set of crystal chandeliers.

Turning the corner of our own street, we found the family out in pairs looking for us, all dressed in their Shabbos clothes. They were running in and out of the closemouths calling: 'Wally, Ebby . . . Where are you? *ANSWER*!'

Jacky the jumbo boy was the first to spot us. 'Hey, you two! What's up? We've been everywhere looking for you. Ma's very angry. It's nearly yom-tov.'

'We were lost,' shouted Wally. 'But it's all right now.

33

We've got enough money for the pictures on Saturday. I'll treat you.'

'You'll get treated when Ma catches you,' grumbled Jumbo, irritated at missing the fabulous tip. When we got home, there was Ma all adorned in her best black silk dress, clipped high at the neck with a cameo brooch, her bare white arms as lovely as ever. Only the roughness of her hands and her worn-down feet revealed her hard work.

The room which, only yesterday, had served as a grocer's store had been reassembled. It was a transformation. There stood our enormous round table covered with a sparkling white cloth. Tall candles were lit and the table spread with all kinds of delicacies, nuts, wine, and matzo.

In the centre of the table on a tray stood four glasses of wine which are specified in the *Haggadah*, the Book of Passover. On drinking the four cups one leans to the left side, as it was the custom in ancient times among free noblemen, who used to dine on couches in a leaning position.

A filled glass, remaining untouched, adorned the middle of the tray, destined for Elijah the Prophet.

The table was set in the traditional way with greens, parsley, celery, and the like. Also with bitter herbs to be dipped in vinegar in remembrance of the bitterness of our exiled lives. Nuts mixed with wine commemorated the loam mixed with straw out of which our forefathers had to make bricks for Pharaoh's buildings: the shank-bone and the egg of eternity, slightly burnt, symbolized the Passover lamb and the festive sacrifice, offered during the existence of the temple in Jerusalem on the eve of the festival.

An appetizing aroma from the kitchen reminded Wally and me that we'd had nothing to eat for half a day. Ma was so relieved to see us she forgot to be angry. 'Vey's mere. I thought something happened to you. Where you been?' And without waiting for an answer, she blamed herself. 'I shouldna have sent two wee wuns like you so far.'

'The man said everything was all right, Ma.' We gazed up

at her in awe. She had never looked so good to me. 'Och, never mind. There's always someting to worry from,' she sighed. 'Go get your good clothes on. It's time for Sader.'

I knew that Ma was glad to see us back. Yet in all my childhood days I never remember her kissing us or showing any physical signs of love. We gave our hands a quick lick of the sponge and changed into our Shabbos clothes. Around the huge circular table my entire family was seated. Every place, every person so spick and span. All their young faces shining.

I recall once on a shopping message, Mrs Teitelbaum the baker's wife enquired of me, as she wrapped the baigles, 'Aren't you one of those Cowan children? What a big family you have!'

'Yes,' I sighed, weary from years of such questions, 'eight girls and three boys.' Mrs Teitelbaum handed me the paper bag. 'How do you remember all their names?' she asked.

Can I ever forget them? Slowly my eyes swivelled round the Passover table. Over there sat my sister Tilly the toiler. A title well earned by our hard-working eldest sister. Next to her was our quiet domesticated Rose, by any other name just as sweet. Then Lily, like her namesake of the valley, born to die in full bloom. There sat Rachel, a wide-eyed, dark, impulsive beauty, as though she had just stepped out of the pages of the Old Testament.

Next to her came George, the first boy after four daughters. The apple of his mother's eyes, he was Ma's own version of Sonny Boy and always called 'Sonny'. After that our bespectacled Kate, striving to be called sophisticated Kitty, which she thought more in the image of the intelligent flapper of that time.

Then came Rina, our lovely Juliet at age fifteen, being courted by her Romeo. Not under a balcony in Verona, but in a back close in the Gorbals. Truly they were a pair of star-crossed lovers. Next there sat Annie, a dark, lively, laughing Renoir painting of a girl. Over there was Jacky, whose rugged appearance belied his sensitive nature. Who could foresee the future war medals on his broad chest?

Now Wally, our eternal reluctant schoolboy, forever wending his unwilling way to school. At last myself aged eight, sometimes called 'Charlie's Aunt', because there sitting beside me was my nephew of that name, only one year my junior.

As was the custom, the first-born son George conducted the service of the evening. He lifted the dish containing the matzo, the bone of the lamb and the egg and removed it from the table saying: 'This is the bread of affliction, which our ancestors ate in the wilderness; let all that are hungry enter and eat; and all who are in want, come and celebrate the Passover. This year we celebrate it here, but next year we hope to celebrate in the land of Israel. This year we are bondsmen here, but next year we hope to be freemen.'

The family rose and thanked God for our blessings. Especially the fact that the Red Sea had opened up and allowed us to escape from the Egyptians. George filled the second cup of wine and put the dish again on the table. The youngest person of the immediate family (in this case myself) should then stand up and address the father of the house. But as I had no father, I turned to my big brother George and said: 'Father, may I ask you the four questions? Wherefore is this night distinguished from all other nights? On all other nights we may eat either leavened or unleavened bread, but on this night only unleavened. On all other nights we may eat any species of herbs, but on this night only bitter herbs. On all other nights we do not dip even once, but on this night twice. On all other nights we may eat and drink either sitting or leaning, but on this night we all must lean . . .' I went on as taught in Hebrew school.

The family stood up and responded, reading from the prayer book: 'Because we were slaves unto Pharaoh in Egypt, and the Eternal, our God, brought us forth thence with a mighty hand and an outstretched arm. And if He had not brought forth our ancestors from Egypt, we and our children and children's children had still continued in the bondage to the Pharaohs in Egypt.'

Then I was instructed to open the front door to allow the Prophet Elijah (the Herald of Messianic redemption) to enter and sip his cup of wine. An eerie shiver ran through me when I felt he passed me at the door. I ran back to the table and watched, fascinated, as I thought the wine receded in the glass. My mother informed me that Elijah had partaken of the wine and I returned through the lobby and closed the door. My childish heart felt happy that the Angel had blessed my family for another year.

We chanted Passover songs, stuffed our stomachs with good food and wine until we were very merry. George played a traditional Passover game with us, of hiding a special matzo called the 'affy-cowmin'. During the evening the child who found it received a prize. When there was a lull, I could hear sounds of revelry from other Jewish homes in the building. This happy unforgettable evening was drawing to its end.

Now the girls were faced with the source of nearly all their quarrels – the gigantic washing-up of dishes. 'Come on, Katie,' said Ma. 'We must get the dishes done. The younger keender are tired. You and Rina get started.' Katie did not move from the table. We were all drowsy with the food and the lateness of the hour. Ma gave us angry looks. 'Come on now, move.'

Indeed the wine had taken its effect on our unaccustomed young minds. 'Come on KKKKKatie. BBBBBbeautiful Katie,' sang Jacky and Wally. 'You're the only gggggirl that we adore.'

'You'll get a crack on the ear, you kids,' said Katie. 'And anyway you know . . .' She stood up in her short beaded dress and adjusted the monocle she had acquired for the evening. 'I don't answer to any other name but Kitty.' The boys laughed. 'KKKKkitty, bbbbeautiful Kitty . . .' their voices trailed off. Kitty started laughing too. Her bark, as usual, was worse than her bite. 'Listen, you kids. Get moving. I'm laughing now, but I'm angry.' I moved forward to stand close to her and show her I was near. The two of us started to clear the table.

But Kate was muttering to me '. . . anyway when I grow up, I won't have all this nonsense. What's it all for, after all? Passover?' Kate rattled the cutlery. 'Just a lot of work for women. That's all.'

This last remark angered Ma, who was standing nearby sorting dishes. Ma swung Katie round by the shoulders. She turned her into the suddenly hushed room. Ma's face turned red-hued with suppressed rage. 'You hear what she say? She won't bother with all dis. She won't bother with God or with all that nonsense.'

Letting go of the now thoroughly sorry Katie, Ma turned to all of us. 'I don't care who you are or what you are. All of you.' Ma whipped off her spectacles and wiped the steam of anger from them. 'Do you hear? Suppose you're a Christian Goy or a Yiddisher. What would we all be without something to believe in. You know what? You know what we would be?'

She never waited for an answer, but went on, 'Yes, I know. Without God, without religion, we would all be just a shteek flaish mit agen [a piece of flesh with eyes in it]!'

Suddenly there was a great clatter of dishes as we all ran to do the washing-up.

THE ISLAND OF DREAMS

So that was April. I tore another leaf off my odd little calendar, threw it out of the window, and away fluttered another page of my young life down Apsley Place.

With my new page marked 'MAY', I began to pencil off the days until I saw Ma bringing out the old wicker hampers. Then I did not need a calendar to know it was summer.

The PS *Kylemore* was not so much an old battered paddle steamer as a legend on the Clyde. It left the Broomielaw, Glasgow about 1.30 p.m. every day and, if you were lucky, chugged into Rothesay around five in the afternoon. Heroically the old craft had fought its way through the First World War back to the holiday-makers of the Clyde coast.

About twelve noon on 1 June 1929, a strange safari could be seen rounding the corner of Bridge Street on its approach to Broomielaw wharf. At its head came Ma, a straw basket tucked under each arm, a shabby black patent shopping-bag and two children attached to each wrist. From all her bags protruded round loaves of sweet and sour bread, cucumbers, herrings, sandwiches, cakes, and bottles of milk.

Following behind were the older members of the family, between each pair of them a large battered trunk. Behind them marched a few stalwart youths of the neighbourhood, who were promised sixpence each to carry the heavier and still endless hampers, which were to be deposited in the hold of the ship.

The reason for all the luggage, apart from clothing for so many people, was that Ma would not use a dish, a piece of cutlery, or a pot that had touched non-Jewish food. So most of the hampers contained all her own kitchen utensils, table and bed linen. On top of all this we had to carry stocks of drapery to sell to the unsuspecting islanders.

Boarding the steamer, Ma went straight to the bow, where wooden front benches were free with your ticket. Otherwise you paid for the hire of a deck chair. The larger luggage was secured down below. All she had left was her food bundles, cases for her momentary need, and the inevitable horde of children.

Immediately the boat left the pier, we children felt terrible pangs of hunger. It made no difference that we had not long risen from our home table. In the midst of the jostling passengers, Ma had to get out her big bread-knife and the thick loaves of black bread. She held the loaf across her chest in a most suicidal manner and cut the slices. Then spread them with jam. While we were munching and drinking our milk, the River Clyde lapped along beside us. I read slowly to Ma every name of every famous shipyard. Her hand shading her eyes from the sun, she blinked at the men up high. Any kind of skilled work aroused her admiration. Always she used to say in Yiddish: 'Arbeit macht dem leben zeest [work makes your life sweet].' This was one of her truer axioms. If only a quarter of her little sayings had come true, what a sweet life she would have had!

A little while later I felt the boat heaving under me. Even my strong eight-year-old stomach could not digest black bread, bananas, and pickled cucumbers.

'I'm feeling sick, Ma.'

'Och, not again? Don't start that. There's nuttin wrong with you. Here, run about and zoop in the feesh air.'

I did this for a while, and it worked quite well. Further down the river opened out into the Firth. 'Look Ma! There's a two-yellow-funnel boat. Why don't we go on it? It's much faster. Ours has only one black-and-white funnel.'

'Och, that's for train and boat people. We can't affort it. It's cheaper to go "all-the-way" like we do.'

Sailing by was the aristocracy of the Clyde paddle fleet. They made a colourful array of slim red funnels and double white chimneys. There, gliding through the water, was the

King Edward VII, Eagle III, the *Duchess of Fife*, and the *Queen Alexandra*.

But the veteran *Kylemore* puffed arrogantly on her unhurried way. 'All tickets, please,' I heard the Purser cry. This was the moment we had been dreading. For my mother had bought only one adult and one child's ticket, although there must have been at least twelve of our family and relatives aboard the crowded ship. 'Have your tickets ready, please.'

The Purser clicked the little pincer he carried for punching holes in the pasteboard. Jacky gave me a nudge, whispering, 'Make for the Ladies' Room. Wally and I will run for the Gents.' We scampered like well-fed hamsters over the deck, past the brass-buttoned officer, and down the hatchway. As I sat in the rest-room I could hear the band pounding away – 'Happy days are here again' – on an upper deck.

I felt that I would never see a happy day again. The lady in charge was quite unsuspicious. She even gave me a chocolate biscuit. This did not help my squeamishness. I panicked often, wondering when to go up.

I imagined the family had gone off without me. When I reckoned the danger might be over, I sauntered up on deck. Everything seemed to be sailing along splendidly. Just then Jacky ran up. 'Wally has dropped his shoe into the engine. It's somewhere down there. What will we do? Suppose the boat breaks down?'

My mother, followed by her entire entourage, made for the engine-room. Wally stood on a greasy iron platform, gingerly holding one shoeless foot. He nearly followed his luckless piece of footwear downward when he saw Ma approaching.

'My goo'ness. What next?' she cried. 'Can you see it? Can you get it back?'

'Gosh, no. I'm afraid it's gone for ever,' said Wally tearfully. 'Shall I call the man?'

'No, no,' Ma replied hurriedly. 'Don't make attention to yourself. You know about the tickets. You'll just hop off with me when the time comes.'

Our large family was a bit crowded on that small space. Such an uproar would surely bring officialdom down on us. Chug, chug, chug, the platform vibrated. I wondered what would happen next. Would the shoe choke the engine? Would we all be drowned? I shivered with fear. Our crowd broke up hastily at the sight of a peaked cap.

We all streamed up on deck. The *Kylemore* was now on its approach run towards Rothesay pier. Lying as though it had just been dropped down amongst the hills, the bay shimmered like a massive blue-gold jellyfish. The tips of its tentacles reaching out to flop on odd strips of beach here and there.

High above the harbour towered the town itself. Rothesay, on our island of dreams, to whose enfolding beauty I unfailingly return feasting my eyes anew. The steamer tied up at the pier. Our landing was imminent. Walter had been allocated a ticket in order not to draw attention to his limping shoeless figure.

Jacky and I and some of the others, slipped through the crowded gangway. When questioned by the jaunty-capped Purser – 'Hey, you, wee girl! Where's your ticket?' I jerked my thumb over my shoulder. 'My mother's coming just behind, sir.'

I pushed my way through the crowd, stepped on to the pier, heaving a sigh of relief. Jacky had still to come. 'Here, you, boy. Where's your ticket?' Jacky jerked his thumb over his shoulder. 'My mother's coming behind with it.'

Quickly he jostled down the gangway. On the pier, Ma called the roll of the younger children. 'Katie, Rina, Annie, Jacky, Walter, Evelyn.'

All offspring and packages were accounted for. The sun glinted on the metal locks of my ancient suitcase. One or two drivers offered their horse-drawn cabs for hire. But Ma had no money for such luxuries. We marched along the promenade in our usual voortrekker style.

At the end of the Ardbeg shore, the Siamese-twin villas of

Libya and Senga awaited us. There, astride his front step, stood Mr Andrew Bone, a tall, spare, bristling, military-looking man. He seemed aghast at this invasion of his property. Granted he had rented one of his houses to us. But he had never anticipated this Rabelaisian mob.

As it turned out, he was not nearly so fierce as his appearance led one to expect. He was rather shyly afraid of children. And, as our friendship grew, he confided to me that he had never been in the wars. And that Senga was merely the name of his wife Agnes spelled backwards. I was fascinated by this secret and went about for weeks looking for words that made sense spelt backwards.

At any rate, Libya was our home for the summer. We filled every corner of the old rambling house with fun and laughter. Through the wall in Senga, the childless Bones went about their neat rooms in quiet complacency.

They were bounded on their side of the garden by a red bricked manse. Our garden wall was the end of all habitation. When we jumped over this wall we very soon found ourselves in the heart of the Skeoch woods. This led to many adventures.

When I gazed out from our attic bedroom window, across the bay, the mist lifted its veil and the mountains of Argyll drew themselves up majestically in front of me.

BETTY THE HEN

The morning after our arrival, my sisters went about their business. Lily had already made some contacts. Parcels were ready for delivery. The other girls set out for Largs, Gourock, and Dunoon. Stripped to the waist, Jacky, Wally, and I went fishing from the rocks, or swimming from the open bathing station. We appointed ourselves unpaid seamen, helping to dispatch the *May Queen* on its hourly trips round the bay.

One day in that summer of 1929 my mother made an important discovery. We were not the only Jewish family on the Island of Bute. In the course of one of her shopping expeditions into Rothesay, she made the acquaintance of Mrs Nubilsky, whose husband ran a bicycle and pram-renting shop just opposite the putting green.

An equally important part of the conversation proved to be the fact that Mr Nubilsky was an accredited shochet, a man qualified to kill animals according to the laws of the Jewish religion. Ma was delighted to hear this. Because of the distance from our kosher butchers in Glasgow, the purchase of fresh meat created a major problem. Non-kosher food never entered our home. She permitted herself to buy newly-caught fish from the boats that tied up in the harbour. Milk and eggs were delivered from a farm nearby.

One of my married sisters occasionally loaded a parcel of egg loaves from the bakers in the Gorbals on to the old *Kylemore*. With this we made do. But Ma had an irresistible urge to make real Shabbos dinner with chicken soup and all the trimmings. Off we went to see Mr Cross the poultry-farmer. I trotted along beside Ma. My small schoolgirl figure and her tall bulky shape threw contrasting shadows on the sunlit hedges.

It was a shimmering hot June day. And in all the years that have passed since then, memory makes it more brilliant each time I remember it.

Rolling heavily in her almost bandy walk, Ma trudged up the hot dusty farm road. 'This heat is firing my bunions,' she winced. Towards the end she limped badly. She adjusted her worn black leather shopper on her arm and shouted to a big rugged red-haired man. 'Goot morning. Are you Mr Cross?' He touched his cap. 'Morning, missis. Yes, I am.'

'I'm the woman from Libya on the Ardbeg Road. I get all my eggs here.' Hens were clucking all around us. 'Oh, yes.' His freckled hand wiped the perspiration from his brow. 'I mind now. You're the lady with all those nice-looking daughters.'

Ma threw him a suspicious look. 'Never mind that. Have you got a good fat hen for sale?'

'Sure we have. But I don't usually sell 'em this way.' Mr Cross laughed. 'Going to start a farm in opposition to me?'

'No, tanks. I got plenty to do. I just want someting for the weekend dinner.' I scarcely listened to all this, enveloped as I was in my mother's long skirt. At first I peeped out in fear and then courageously put my hand out to touch the strutting parade. Ma ran her eyes over the noisy farmyard. 'Hey! There's a nice fat one.' She pointed to a lovely white regal-looking bird. 'How about that one?'

Mr Cross ran over and grabbed it. 'It looks aa right to me. I don't see why you shouldnie have it.' Ma poked around in her purse. 'Well, just tell me how much it is, and I'll take it.'

'OK,' said the farmer. 'I'll go up the road to the house and gauge its weight, and then I'll wring its neck for you.'

'Don't do that, please,' Ma pleaded hurriedly. 'Say how much. And I'll take it in my shopping bag.'

'You mean, you want it alive, missis?'

'Yes, please, Mr Cross. Just tie some string round its legs. And I'll pop it in the bag.'

As we rolled along the road home, I tried to help with

45

the heavy bag. I put my hand up to lift an end. The hen's innocent blue eyes gazed down into mine. It was love at first sight. I called her Betty.

As I have said, I was the youngest of a poor widow's family. And it may sound incredible, but it is quite true when I say that I never possessed a doll or, for that matter, a toy of any description. There was no lack of love in our home. I felt safe and secure always. I loved my mother deeply. But she was just there, like the sun and the moon and the clouds in the sky, taken for granted.

Everyone fondled and cuddled me, the baby. I was bathed, romped, and loved by all the older sisters and brothers. I longed for something of my very own. Betty the Hen was my first true love. She fulfilled my need. Within a few hours my two brothers, Wally and Jacky, made a little wooden hut surrounded by a wire pen for my pet. I painted the name 'Betty' in dark blue on white wood.

After meals, I brought out scraps of food for her. I even tried to clean and brush Betty's feathers. The bird seemed to thrive on all this attention. Her feathers looked whiter, her stature more regal than before. She clucked happily (I thought) whenever she saw me approaching. We gazed into each other's eyes. I said little. Young love does not need much conversation.

Betty had been bought from the farm on a Monday. On Thursday, Ma sent a message to Mr Nubilsky's house above the bicycle shop, to say his services were required that evening.

My two brothers and myself were out picking brambles for jam in the Skeoch woods all day Thursday. It had been a happy, carefree day. We were exhausted from the heat. I knew that Betty was well stocked with food and water. So I did not go round the back yard. We flopped into our threesome bed, and I lapsed into a heavy childish sleep.

The next morning, Friday, before breakfast, I discovered the little hut was empty. Not a sound from the yard. All was silence. I ran into the kitchen. 'Ma, for goodness, Ma. The hen's gone.'

Feathers flew in all directions. My mother was busy plucking. 'Ach, here it is. Surely you knew I wanted it for Shabbos dinner. As soon as it is cleaned, I will kosher it and start it in the big pot. For tomorrow is Sabbath . . . Saturday.'

I could not raise my eyes further to the bleeding mass on her lap. Surely that was not Betty! Feeling sick, I raced across the promenade to the shore. I threw pebbles aimlessly in the water. Small waves rippled back at me. I thought of my make-believe puppy and the old stray cat I'd wanted for my own. Yet I never dreamed of begging for Betty's life. We were a large, hungry family. Although I had deluded myself for a short time, I knew in my young-old heart that Betty was for eating. I kicked my thinly-clad foot against a rock until my toes almost bled.

On Saturday morning I awakened on a pillow of grief. It was Shabbos, a quiet day, when no rough games were allowed. You had to keep your clothes in Sunday-best condition. Time dragged by. At last I heard my mother's voice echoing across the promenade. 'Children, keender, come on, now! Wash your hands and get ready for Shabbos dinner.'

We filed into the seldom-used dining room. Each child went to his or her place. After Kiddush wine and a little prayer murmured by all, we were served steaming plates of chicken soup with little knaidle doughballs dancing about on the surface. I turned away from this, the fragrant essence of my love. Then came the main course. This was stuffed roast chicken carried in on a large platter surrounded by 'cholent' brown potatoes and green vegetables.

Eagerly plates were pushed at Ma from both sides of the long table.

'I like the leg,' shrilled Wally.

'Give me the wing,' cried Jacky.

Cannibals! I raged into myself. My own brothers, too! Uninvited, a piece of white meat appeared in front of me. I blinked down at it. My tears made a gravy on the plate.

SOME ROTHESAY PEOPLE

My sister Lily, perceptive and kind as always, suspected my grief; and, in an effort to comfort me, she promised to take me along on her rounds on Monday morning. I loved meeting people, as long as I did not have to make the first overtures. So off I went with my sister on her Monday morning business rounds.

Lily's charming knack of making friends while she went about her business had to be seen to be believed. Her best friend in Rothesay was Mrs Fornari, the huge fat dark-haired Scots-born wife of a wee thin Italian chap. This unlikely but happily-married couple ran a café and sweetie shop in Rothesay away up near the recreation grounds.

The café was always full of people. But many an evening Lily found a quiet corner in the sanctuary of the back-shop kitchen, where she and Mrs Fornari sat drinking gallons of black coffee. They had a lot in common. Both of them were easy-going and good-natured. Neither of them had ever cared for tea. They were both happily wed to contrasting yet deeply compatible partners. And they could commiserate with each other for hours over the fact that neither had ever had a child.

Bella Fornari's shop was the hub of the High Street. Not only did she purvey ice-cream, lemonade, tea, and biscuits, but she served out homely platitudes, sound advice, and small sums of money which she knew full well she would never get back. While Lily and Bella were having their *tête-à-tête* evenings, Arturo Fornari would wander in and out of the kitchen, between the steady tinkle of his cash register and the comings and goings of his customers.

He always had a few words to add to the conversation.

Bella beamed at him lovingly, treating him like a small clever son. Everything he said was wonderful and worth listening to. Arturo smiled and looked her over pleasantly. And their bantering affectionate chatter easily revealed their happy state.

Characteristically, Lily was not averse to doing business even when she was out for pleasure. And that Monday morning Lily had the pleasure of my company while she conducted her business in Fornari's back shop. Arturo came in and said, 'Lily, I tol' you abou' thissa woman wass asking for some blankets for her beds. You wanna see her?'

'Oh, yes, certainly,' replied Lily. 'If you know her, and you recommend her. Send her in.' I was sitting in the back shop of the café sucking an ice-cream cone while Bella and Lily sipped their coffee. Mrs McQuirk was ushered in. She looked at Mrs Fornari, but pointed her finger at my sister.

'Is this the wee drapery woman?'

'Yes,' said Bella. 'This is Lily, and this is Mrs McQuirk.' The two women nodded to each other. Mrs McQuirk was a small grey shrivelled woman with tight dried lips. She made a little putting noise at the end of every other word as her lips came together. From her there wafted a strong odour which I could not quite identify.

'Well. It's like this, Lily. I'm needing some-*pp*-blankets. For ma summer people are arrivin-*pp*-on Saturday. I like to pay cash . . .' Lily raised her eyebrows. I knew she had heard that one before. 'But . . .' went on Mrs McQuirk, 'am a bit short this time of the year. So am askin ye to tak me on as a customer.'

'All right,' replied Lily promptly. 'Bella here recommended you . . .'

'Oh, aye,' interrupted Mrs Fornari, 'ye're aa right there, Lily. I'll stake my life on Mrs McQuirk. Your money's as good as in the bank wi her.'

Bella was always staking her life on somebody's honesty. And for all the many times she might have lost it, she never lost her faith in human nature. 'OK,' Lily nodded, 'I'll be glad to help you. What's your order?'

Mrs McQuirk ran her bony finger over her cracked lips. 'Well. It's like this,' she hesitated. 'I think-*pp*-am needin two pair of Ayrshire blankets. But maybe you'd come and give me some advice, eh! My house is just on the front facing the pier. Number Eleven, Bute Crescent.'

'OK. I'll be round in the morning. And we'll talk it over,' said Lily.

The next morning I volunteered to help Lily with her bulky parcel. We set out for Mrs McQuirk's house opposite the pier. Climbing the two flights of stairs, we pulled the bell and were admitted by our prospective customer. As soon as I stepped into the kitchen, I realized what the odour was that clung to her. It was the smell of cats. The house was pervaded with the stench. The cats were all over the kitchen. There must have been more than a dozen of them. They were lying in baskets by the fire. Some were sitting on chairs. One was relaxing in the kitchen sink. Another had just vomited some grey sick into a saucer. And yet another purred on the kitchen table alongside a loaf of bread.

'Would your wee sister like a piece and jam?' Mrs McQuirk enquired of Lily. 'Oh, no thank you,' I shuddered. Lily pretended to ignore the state of the kitchen. She put the parcel down on the wooden table and started to pull off the string in order to show the goods to Mrs McQuirk. 'Now, Mrs McQuirk,' Lily said with the voice of experience, 'I brought these best-quality Ayrshire blankets. And, if you like, I'll measure your beds. You seemed not too sure about things yesterday.'

All around us were cats rubbing against our legs. One large grey tabby was already purring contentedly on Lily's clean new blankets. Mrs McQuirk examined the parcel of bed clothes. 'Aye. They look fine.' She fingered the wool. 'But I've been thinkin things over since yesterday.'

My spirits plunged downwards as I thought my sister had

51

lost the order. Lily glanced over at Mrs McQuirk. She was quite used to this sort of set-back. 'Well,' went on Mrs McQuirk. 'When I came home last night, I got everything ready for my holiday lodgers. I washed all the old blankets from my cats' baskets. And I've put them on the beds.'

Lily shrugged her shoulders, pushed the old tabby off her new goods, and made as though to wrap up the parcel again. 'But wait a minute.' Mrs McQuirk held Lily's arm. 'They're so temptin.' She fingered the wool again. 'Lovely new blankets.' Mrs McQuirk scratched her head, then made her decision. 'I think,' she went on. 'I think I'll tak the two new pair for my cats' baskets.'

Another great Rothesay friend of my sister Lily was old Granny MacArthur. Lily told me that she met Granny in the ordinary way when she was knocking round the doors looking for new customers. It was a pouring wet day, weather well known to Rothesay. The old lady came to the door of her cottage. Lily was a sorry sight, soaked to the skin, her bedraggled curls clinging to her moist face.

'Hivvens, lassie! Whit are ye sellin in this damp weather? Ye'll catch your death of cold. Come away in and I'll mak ye a cup of hot tea.' In went Lily and sat by the fire. They blethered on. Lily told Mrs MacArthur about Ma and the family, and how we came to be living in Rothesay.

Old Granny MacArthur was greatly interested in our family. She gave Lily a big order for sheets and blankets. In the years that followed, she and Lily became great friends. On a winter's day, old Granny always had a soft boiled egg, hot toast, and a pot of tea waiting for Lily or any of my sisters who called for the money.

When we lived in Rothesay in the summer, Granny MacArthur invited Ma to tea. But Ma politely refused, as she had never taken a cup to her lips in a non-Jewish home. The old Scots granny respected Ma for keeping to her religion.

My mother and Granny MacArthur never set eyes on each

other, ever. Through my sisters they exchanged little gifts. The old granny would knit a fancy tea-cosy and send it along to Ma. Then my mother would bake her a ginger-cake, for she had heard that the old lady loved home baking.

One by one my family were taken up and introduced to Granny MacArthur. She had a beautiful, spotlessly clean home in a neat row of cottages not far from the seafront. Her fire burned brightly. Over the mantelpiece hung a picture of her three sons, one of whom had been drowned at sea. The other two lived in Canada and sent her regular cheques for her housekeeping.

Granny was always dressed in black, with a white lace collar clutched tightly round her throat. Her face was thin, but creamy and fresh; and, though she never went out of the house, her feet were always shod in high black buttoned boots. Over eighty she was, as I remember her, for ever sitting erect in a straight-backed chair with her fine silvery head held high and proud.

One day, Lily escorted my sister Annie and myself to tea with Granny MacArthur. I hadn't wanted to go. I was terrified of old age. It reminded me of death, which I didn't want to think about. I imagined that a person of her age would surely collapse and die in front of my childish eyes. My teenage sister Annie was just beginning to use powder and lipstick. She was all dressed and made up for the afternoon out. Old Granny MacArthur opened the door of her cottage. 'Come awa in,' she said over and over again as she ushered us into her shining kitchen.

We all sat down. We were an odd quartet: the old ramrod lady, Lily smartly in her prime, Annie the pert teenager, and myself a frightened eight-year-old. A little table was set by the fire for tea, with delicate china cups and a platter of melting hot scones.

Lily and Annie made themselves comfortable. I edged away as far as I could from the old lady. I hoped she would not notice me. As she was pouring out the tea, Granny suddenly clattered down the teapot. Grabbing Lily's arm, and pointing to Annie, old Granny screamed, 'My Gode! Whit's that on her mooth?' Lily looked at Annie's lipsticked mouth. But before she could answer, the old lady snatched a lace hankie out of her pocket and made towards Annie.

'She's bleedin! Hurry up, Lily, and help me. Your sister's bleedin to death!' Annie started to cry as the old woman came towards her. I jumped behind my chair and cowered there. But Lily caught the wink of Granny MacArthur's eye. The two of them looked at each other and went into uncontrollable peals of laughter.

I vowed to myself that I would never go back there. I'm sure Annie felt the same. But, as we were leaving, the old lady slipped a pound note into each of our hands. She smiled down at me from her great age. 'Dinna be feart o me, lassie. We're all goin the same road. One day when you're auld like me . . .' She laid her hand lightly on my shoulder, then emphasized her words, '. . . and ye will be, lassie. Ye will be. Ye'll understaun it's better to finish wi a wee joke.'

Now, Mr Trescowthick was another friend of Lily's. Although I have used many pseudonyms in this book, that was his real name. He was the keeper of the pier gates. He used to take care of my sisters' heavy cases and parcels, by keeping them in his office during the day, for an hour or two. It relieved the girls to make a few calls unencumbered. Then they would come back for their cases later on. He also let us children on to the pier for nothing. A great saving of a penny, when we met the *Kylemore* for our food parcels from Glasgow.

Mr Trescowthick was a small, hunchbacked cripple. We later discovered that his wife was a bedridden invalid. I suppose they were not always like that. But somehow I could not picture him as a young man. Still, he was the soul of kindness and taught my brothers much about bait for fishing off the pier-end at night.

My mother sent his wife all sorts of tasty morsels as a

'thank you' for his kindness to us. And Mr Tress, as we called him, acquired quite a taste for baigles and coochons, our Jewish morning rolls. But Ma would have been shocked if she had seen him eating such very kosher bread with a large piece of bacon in the middle.

I did not become so friendly with Mr Tress as I did with my particular friend Mr Waldrey. I first met Wilson Waldrey when my sisters Lily and Rae treated the family to an evening cruise up to Ardrishaig. They always gave us children a happy time with lots of ice-cream and chocolate bars. We had confidence to enjoy ourselves, because my sisters, unlike my mother, bought the correct number of tickets on the boat. So we could look any officer, on that steamer, straight in the face.

It was a perfect summer's evening. Not a breath of a breeze to ruffle Lily's curly hair. I leaned out and over the rail. The bow of the steamer cut confidently through the mirror-like surface of the water. A few minutes earlier the deck had been alive with shrieking playing children. Then a sudden peace held the balmy evening air.

Across the deck behind me came the sound of a piano. Silence descended on the noisy passengers. Only the sweet deep playing could be heard. Perhaps it was the charm of the evening with the stars twinkling overhead, but the playing seemed to be so much better than before. We were held in a suspended cloud of music for a few minutes.

When he was finished, the solo pianist from the four-man-band got up and, while the band played on, came across collecting pennies in his little black velvet bag. This was Mr Waldrey. He was a man, then in his late forties, slim and slight in every way. I think the word that best fitted him was 'gentle'. I saw a thin brown face with tiny fine lines running over it, a gentle smile and a pair of deep kind eyes.

Lily and I were together at the rail. She clung to the edge of my tunic so that I would not fall to a watery grave. Mr Waldrey held out the velvet bag, his eyes carefully avoiding it and fixing themselves on me. I fished in my skirt pocket and came up with my childish wealth – one ha'penny – feeling embarrassed and trying to hide it.

My sister Lily knew the pianist, as she knew so many people on the boats and in the town of Rothesay. She smiled and pushed some money into his bag. 'Hullo,' said Lily. 'How's your wife?' He smiled. 'She's well, thanks. Is this your family?'

'Yes,' replied Lily. 'We're just taking the kids for a cruise up the Kyles. My mother will get a quiet evening to herself for a change.' Something made me speak up. 'Your music's awfully good,' I said, daringly for me. 'Much better than I've heard before on the boats.' Now the crowds were milling all around us. 'Oh!' he was surprised. 'You're a bit of an expert, then, for a wee girl?'

'Not really,' I said hurriedly.

'That one,' Lily indicated me, 'has a mind of her own, I can tell you.'

'Well, I know what I like,' said I.

'That's a good start anyway,' Mr Waldrey interposed.

'I liked that last tune,' I said. 'It didn't sound a bit like "Sailing doun the watter" or that sort of thing.' He smiled wistfully, 'I hope not. That was Chopin.'

I had no idea what he meant by that. It sounded like chopped pan – a loaf – or something. From the soft clipped way he spoke, I guessed he was an Englishman who had lived some length of time in Scotland. All this time he held the collecting bag at his side, and I did my best not to look at it. There was something about that humble bag. His kind gentle eyes held mine. I shook myself out of those eyes.

Mr Waldrey continued on his way round the deck, jingling the pennies in the bag to attract attention. Hardly anyone looked at him as they poked the coins in. Mr Waldrey wandered back towards us. 'You know,' he said, looking straight at me. 'I don't know why I'm telling you this. Perhaps it's because you remind me of my own little girl. But my life is in music. I know nothing else. I've tried everything and always come back to my piano.'

'I think I understand,' I muttered. Not knowing how to take his confidence. He added quite simply, 'I am a musician.' I nodded emphatically, 'You certainly are.' Waldrey handed me a card. 'Perhaps you'd like to visit me sometime. Your sister knows where I stay. Come along and hear me play one day . . . And, you know,' he tweaked my nose, 'my wife makes the nicest treacle scones.'

When I showed Lily the man's scribbled card, she said it was all right for me to go. Mrs Waldrey was a customer of our business, so Lily knew the couple well. The scrawled address was almost unreadable. And one afternoon I found myself taking many wrong turnings up the hot tarry zig-zag roads of the serpentine avenues overlooking Rothesay Bay. At last I found the correct door in the building where they lived.

In answer to my knock, the door was opened by a well-built grey-haired woman. Her longish yet plump face and high hair style made her look taller than she actually was. I could hardly understand what she said as she called me in. But afterwards I realized she spoke in a thick Yorkshire accent.

'Oo, and who are you, m'dear?' she said in a state of permanent excitement.

'Mr Waldrey said I could call. I met him on the cruise the other night.'

'Oh, yes,' she replied busily. 'Lily's wee sister. Mr Waldrey told me about you.' She looked me over with a sad expression. 'I can see what he meant. You do look like our little girl.' Then she changed back to her busy tone. 'And you like his playing. Coom in, m'dear.'

There was no entrance hall. I stepped right in off the top landing of the close into her living-room. The flat was what is commonly known as a 'single end'. It consisted of only one room containing everything. The lavatory was situated on the stairhead.

I viewed the large room, shabby yet clean, considerably cluttered with many chairs and little tables, a recess bed, two sofas, a grand piano piled high with music and a beautiful gold-painted harp. Underneath the only window, it also had the kitchen sink. 'Sit down, dear,' cooed Mrs Waldrey. 'You must be tired climbing oop all those hills.' I sat down and looked around. 'This is a lovely place you have here,' I said, looking at the musical instruments more than anything else. 'Oo yes. Of course you've never been here before. I forgot. Wait, I'll make some tea and we'll have a weee chat. It's nice having a child visitor. We've no weee ones of our own.'

She said 'wee' in a drawn-out kind of way, emphasizing the word and not taking it naturally as Scots people do. While she flitted about, busy with the tea things, I fingered the gold harp. I had never seen such a magnificent instrument. Mrs Waldrey rattled the cups. 'Your sister told me all about your family. And the more power to you all. Not letting yourselves starve in that terrible Glasgow place.'

'It's not so bad in Glasgow,' I said loyally. 'Though I do like Rothesay very much.'

'Yes, I'm sure you do, dear. Nice fresh air and the sea and all. That's why we like it too.' She beckoned me near to where the table was loaded with bread, jam, and hot buttered scones. While we sipped our tea, she chatted. 'Mr Waldrey plays on the boats all summer now. Things are not too bad. It's the winters that are hard.' Mrs Waldrey rattled on. 'As I told your sister, my husband used to play in the cinemas. But that's all gone with talking pictures now.'

She had acknowledged the fact that I was a child, but she spoke to me as though we were of equal age.

'Anyway,' she sighed, 'we won't worry about the winter until it cooms. Mr Waldrey will be in any minute now. I'm sure he'll be pleased to see you.'

Just as she said this, my friend the musician came quietly through the doorway. He walked towards me. 'Delighted to meet you again, m'dear.' He raised my small outstretched

58

hand and gave me a fine old-world bow, as though I were a duchess. I noticed that the elbows of his jacket were worn through.

After tea, Mr Waldrey said, 'So now, here we have the young lady who likes music.' I blushed. 'Och, I don't know much about it. But I liked your playing that night on the boat.' He smiled gently, 'I could see that. Would you like to hear some more?' I clapped my hands together. 'I'd love to.'

Mr Waldrey fingered through a few bars at the piano. Then he played the piece I'd heard him play on the evening of the cruise. A little thrill of pleasure ran up my spine. He played the piano for a while, then slipped over to the harp and began strumming it. He had a lovely light touch.

His wife sat stiffly in a chair in her best 'listening-to-music' attitude. Her face wore the proud expression of an ordinary woman unaccountably married to a genius.

Summer after summer I visited the Waldreys. We spent wonderful evenings together. He played a little Mozart, Tchaikovsky, Beethoven. His lack of training might perhaps have been obvious to an expert, but I was only a small girl.

Again and again he came back to that Chopin prelude which I first heard him play the evening we met. It haunts me yet. I listened enchanted. He played enraptured. His wife used to look from me to him, nodding and beaming. He told me that he was self-taught and could only just manage to read printed music. They had had an only child, a little girl, who died quite young. During the lean years, when there were too many pianists looking for jobs on the summer boats, he was hired to play the harp. He had never been robust, and I think it was the harp that finally ruined his health.

Wearily he carried it up and down the decks of the ship all day. Then he trailed it along the zig-zag serpentine avenues and up three flights of stairs at the end of each week.

I was still a young woman the last time I saw the Waldreys. But his life was fading. I shall never forget my old friend.

Whenever I hear that Chopin prelude, I picture his gentle fine hands running over the keyboard. The small appreciation of music that I do have, I gleaned from him.

I never saw his wife again after he died. But if she had asked me to write his epitaph, I would have written quite simply:

WILSON WALDREY:
HE WAS A MUSICIAN

I think my old friend would have liked that.

THE SKEOCH WOODS

The holiday town of Rothesay, set like a golden dream of childhood into the sunny hills of the Island of Bute, had much to offer city families on vacation. Amongst its attractions were golf and putting greens, the Winter Gardens theatre, and a real-sea open-air bathing station. The only thing that nature had not provided for the resort was a beach. There was only a small patch of sand, usually crowded, for children to play on.

Although we loved to track in the Skeoch woods, and ride round the bay in the little motor-boats, sooner or later we younger children had an urge to make sandcastles. And so one afternoon in that hot July of 1929, there were five of our family on the overcrowded sands.

The Salvation Army were holding a meeting on the promenade above the beach. A lady in a navy and red-striped uniform came over to our row of sandcastles. Her nice dark bonnet haloed a sweet face. 'Would you children like to join our service?' She addressed herself to my sister Rina, whose cupid face, blue eyes, and golden brown curls were always a natural attraction. Rina's eyes lit up with laughter. She looked over at us, her lips twitching in mirth. We nodded in agreement. 'Come this way, then, boys and girls. Here's a sweetie to wet your throat before we start. We must sing up for Jesus.'

Into ten little Jewish eyes came a twinkle of mischief. We knew full well we were not allowed to sing Christian hymns. But it all looked so tempting: ladies clanging tambourines and cymbals, a wee fat man banging away at a big drum.

We came off the sands. Annie, not too anxiously, tried to restrain us. 'You know Ma will be angry. It's all about Jesus.'

But Annie's dark head was already rolling with uncontrollable giggles.

Rina bubbled with fun as usual. 'They don't know we're Jewish.' So we joined the crowd of children and formed a circle on the promenade. The velvet-voiced lady clapped her hands. 'Now, altogether, children. Do as I do.' And she started to sing:

> *Running over, running over,*
> *My cup's full and running over,*
> *Since the Lord saved me*
> *I'm as happy as can be*
> *'Cos my cup's full and running over.*

The uniformed lady stood in the centre of the circle and whirled her hands round each other as though she were winding a ball of wool. 'Now, when I do that, you all sing the *"running over"* part. And then clap your hands at *"happy as can be"* . . .'

We whirled our hands in gay abandon, singing at the same time, '*Running over, running over*'. Then we danced around clapping in time to the tambourines. '*We're as happy as can be. My cup's full and running over.*'

The Salvation Army lady signalled us to stop. 'Very good, children,' she announced. 'We're now going to form into a line and march along the seafront to the Mission Hall, in Montague Street. Will you all join us there for lemonade and biscuits?'

Jacky gave me a nudge. 'Just try and stop us.' So Rina, Annie, Jacky, Walter, and myself formed up with the other children. The drums went bang. The cymbals clanged. Five pairs of innocent eyes turned heavenwards, we marched along the promenade singing, '*Jesus loves me. Jesus loves me.*'

Lily and Rae, returning from their day's work in Dunoon, loaded down with parcels, were approaching us along the sea-front. They dropped their parcels. 'My goodness,' Rae laughed, 'do you see what I see?' Lily sighed and shook her head. 'It's those kids again.' My two older sisters stood there in amazement as the parade was about to pass by. Then Lily recovered from her surprise. 'Get them out of there before Ma sees them!'

The two sisters left their parcels lying and chased after us. They yanked us out while the parade marched on undisturbed. 'Come on now, you kids,' said Rae. 'Don't you know you're Yiddisher boys and girls?'

'There was nothing wrong with it,' Rina answered, giggling as usual. 'We were only singing and marching.'

'Well,' said Lily, 'if you've so much energy, help us with these bundles. We're tired and hungry. And we want to go home.'

Robbed of our free refreshments, we were in no mood to go quietly home. Annie and Rina were a bit older than Jacky, Walter, and me. They sobered up quickly and lifted the parcels to help the older girls. Jacky, Wally, and I ran on. I shouted, 'We're not going home with you. You'll just tell Ma. Then there'll be a whole row.'

We started to run along the seafront. Rae turned to the others. 'You take my things. I'll catch them all right.'

But when she did catch us, she scooped her arms around us, then laughingly joined our hands with hers, skipping and singing along. Her dark eyes dancing, her black silky hair blowing in the breeze. *'Oh, I do like to be beside the seaside, Oh, I do like to be beside the sea!'*

We accompanied her in the song, dancing along beside her. It was a lovely sunny day. Our happy mood returned. My sister Rae was always ready for a bit of fun. Taken out of school too young, she was already a working girl. But her overgrown schoolgirl spirits readily came to the fore. In her heart she never grew up. Some forty years later, white hair blowing in the breeze, you can see her, with a bunch of grandchildren, skipping along the nearest beach to Beverly Hills, California. To me, she is the quintessence of eternal youth.

Rae swung us children round. We all started dancing backwards, waving to the others. Unnoticed by us, some workmen were tarring the promenade. Before they could shout 'Whoa there!' the four of us tumbled backwards into the warm tar. Plomp! For a minute I lay there all gooey. Then I began to extract myself from the sticky mess. My pink cotton dress was running black. The boys' trouser seats were saturated, their white shirts ruined. Rae, covered as she was in tar, was laughing fit to burst.

We all stood and looked at each other. Now I knew we were really in trouble. Clothes were a very precious item on Ma's budget. The three of us stripped off our outer clothing, leaving only our singlets and pants. Rae was too old for this. She just lifted her skirt and, still laughing, folded it up backwards revealing her tar-stained bloomers.

Four bedraggled figures, we started off along the promenade towards Ardbeg. When we reached the gate of Libya Rae turned in and up the path home.

But Jacky, Wally, and I were too scared. The remnants of our clothes were not even worth bringing back. Standing outside the gate in our underwear we had a conference. Jacky, a big boy for his age, was then twelve. Wally aged eleven and myself three years younger.

'Let's run away into the woods for ever,' suggested Wally. Jacky nodded. 'That's a good idea. There'll be no rows. We'll just not come back.' I nodded my agreement. Unclothed as we were, we entered the little gate of the woods which was adjacent to our house. We could hear voices shouting, 'Come back, you've nothing on.'

This made us run even faster – and faster and faster, not even stopping, but panting and gasping onwards, until finally we were lost in the heart of the Skeoch woods. We could barely see the sun, blotted out as it was by big tall trees. All around us were clumps of thick bushes with little paths running here and there. By which path had we come? That was the question in my mind.

Sitting down on a tree stump to catch our breaths, we tried to form some kind of plan. But it had been a long hard day for me. I started to cry as usual, 'I've had enough. I want to go home.' I was for ever wanting to go home to my mother. 'That's all very well,' reasoned Jacky. 'But how? Which way?'

'Tell you what,' said Wally. 'Let's try any path and see where it leads to. OK?' We trudged up the path to the right. As we came over the bump of its little hill, a wide clearing came into view. Spread out, in this space, we could see a large encampment of old waggons and horse-drawn buggies. An oddly-dressed crowd of people were cooking on an open stove nearby.

We drew a little nearer. 'Stop!' Jacky grabbed my arm. 'Don't go any further. They're tinkers.' I started to cry again. 'Oh, my! That's terrible! They steal children away. We'll never see Ma and the girls again.'

'Och, stop the waterworks.' Wally wiped my face. 'It's better to think what to do.'

'Right enough,' said Jacky. 'We've taken the wrong path. And we must keep our heads and make plans.' The boys were beginning to enjoy themselves. But I could not share their pleasure. I was already saying a tearful farewell to everything I loved. Running through my mind were visions of myself, years later, as a grown-up tinker lady with a horde of raggedy children of my own.

Suddenly a tall rough man pulled away from the group around the camp fire. The man, heavy and bearded, came treading, unbelievably gently, towards us. As he came nearer, I shivered with fear. He looked like our rabbi. No! he looked, to me, like the Messiah they were always preaching about. I stood quite still, hoping my trembling made no noise, only my head turning away from him, from the future.

My whimpers became audible. Wally put his hand over

my mouth. By now, all three of us were losing our taste for adventure. The man stood for a while as though gazing in our direction. Then the rays of the setting sun caught his eyes and he raised his hand. For a little while he stared in our direction. We held our breaths. He turned his back and wandered down the slope to his encampment.

Then Jacky assumed command. 'Now! It's no use all of us staying here, doing nothing. Sooner or later, we'll have to find a way out of these woods . . . This is what we'll do,' Jacky went on. He always wanted to use his Boy Scouts' training. 'I'll go off on my own.' I immediately clung to him. 'Oh, please don't do that! Don't leave us!'

'Och, don't be silly.' He shook me off. 'I'll not leave you for good.' He was a rugged, hefty boy, yet he gripped me gently. His steady grey eyes held my frightened ones. 'Tell you what,' he said. 'I've just thought of something. Remember that game we played one day here. You know. The tracking with the arrows?'

I nodded. 'Yes, I remember.'

'Well. Let's do the same thing again. I'll make little arrows with twigs. And you follow them wherever they point to.' Wally whispered, 'But what if you take the wrong path?'

'I'll just keep trying back and forward,' Jacky whispered in reply. 'And I won't leave the arrows for you until I'm sure I'm on the right path. Trial and error, you see. So all you have to do is to follow the arrow and you'll find me at home.'

By this time, Wally was not too sure about staying behind. Jacky insisted we should carry out his plan. And we bade him a brave farewell. 'Now you must give me a bit of time. Because I'll be going up and down wrong paths till I find the right one. Let's say you give me half an hour.' In the best Baden-Powell tradition, Jacky loped off through the woods away from the tinker camp. But Wally and I had no way of telling the time. We shivered together, in our scanty underwear, under a bush.

'Do you know what?' Wally said, trying to cheer me up. 'Let's count up to five hundred by fives. Ready?' It was a long count, 'Five, ten, fifteen, twenty, twenty-five, thirty . . .' Lamps were being lit in the tinker encampment. We turned our backs on it. It would be just light enough to see the arrows. We ran along for a bit. Nothing to be seen. At last I spotted something.

'Here it is,' I shouted to Wally. 'The first arrow.' At last our spirits rose. There were two little twigs pointing together with one similar running up the centre. Just like a wild Indian arrow in the pictures. After that, every few yards, we found them, lying on tree stumps. Then at the crossroads of every new set of paths, they lay, pointing in the right direction.

Our hearts lightened with every piece of wood we lifted. Within half an hour or so, we were faced with the familiar green hedges of our garden wall, over which we climbed and dreeped down into the safety of our summer home.

Nights were drawing in. I felt a shiver as I ran along, in my thin dress, with some eggs from Mr Cross's farm. We were going home in the morning. I turned to wave goodbye. Far away along the promenade, around the harbour, thousands of fairy lights twinkled back at me . . .

For my family, Rothesay was the turning-point away from poverty. There was just that wee bit more easiness with money. The majority of the islanders were farmers. The townsmen worked on the fishing and passenger boats. The local people let part of their homes to holiday-makers in the summer. Some owned tearooms or hotels.

The people of Rothesay were friendly, good, clean, and decent. We did an honest trade with them. There were few bad debts. At times there was hardship again, but no real poverty. And so for my mother and the family that island of dreams was the beginning of better days. Neither myself nor any of my sisters and brothers ever lost the deep-set fear that poverty would one day engulf us again. But it never did.

On any summer's day, as I sail into Rothesay Bay, if I shade my eyes against the sun, I can still see Lily and Rae: toiling, as they used to do, up the winding High Street, their bodies weighed down with heavy suitcases filled with drapery; then, after work, treating all of us to ice cream in the Tallies' café in Victoria Street facing the sea: Lily and Rae, the young in heart, picnicking, as though we were all children together, on the beach at Ettrick Bay.

Perhaps some of the islanders remember us? Certainly I remember them. For the kind, weatherbeaten faces of the Rothesay folk will live in my heart forever. We returned year after year to the same house, Libya. Each time our family became smaller as marriage took its romantic toll. Wally and I were never so close again as we were that day in the Skeoch woods. The boys were growing up and had started going out with girls. Ma used to say, 'Small keender, small worries. Big children, bigger worries.' With sons of my own, well do I know now the truth of that saying.

By the last day of August 1929, it was time to go home to Apsley Place. Nothing seemed quite the same, we did not sail back to Glasgow on the *Kylemore*. I don't know – maybe Wally's shoe ultimately did some damage to the engine. The old paddle steamer was slower than before. So we caught the red-funnelled turbine steamer TS *St Columba* on her return journey from the Kyles of Bute.

The ship was very late getting into the Broomielaw. Everything looked so different. We had become accustomed to the funny wee single-decker trams in Rothesay. After three months of blue sea and sky, even the tall tramcars rattling along the city streets looked colourless to me.

With that sinking feeling familiar to all returning holiday-makers, we trailed our baggage along through the Gorbals streets. Ma walked at the head of our zig-zaggedy line as usual. Her tall, bending figure looked strangely dejected. I guess she was in need of a holiday.

How quickly the darkness descended upon us! Tilly and

Rose, my married sisters, had cleaned up our home at Number 33. They had lots of food waiting for us. By the time we had eaten a hot supper, washed our sunburnt faces, and measured our summer-grown inches against those of our pale friends in the street, everything was back to normal.

PINK SATURDAY

And the next day was Saturday. Pink, pink Saturday. Sunday stood strict and true. Monday was blue, Tuesday came many-hued. Wednesday seemed pale grey. Thursday brought black-water bathnight. Friday was red, sweaty, worktight. But Saturday was pink, living pink, laughing pink, bright pink Saturday.

I felt a warm glow inside, thinking of the schooldays of the week gone by, knowing it was Saturday morning. Yet there was a chill air in the kitchen. I peered out of the kitchen window. No frost on the ground. It would be too early on the first of September for that. Turning back into the kitchen, I remembered what made it so cold. There was no fire to heat the room. My mother, being orthodox, would not strike a match, let alone light a fire on Shabbos. It seemed that Mrs Crawford, our one and only Christian neighbour, had not arrived to start the fire.

Nearly all the Jewish women who lived in the street had a non-Jewish friend who came in to light the fires for them. The Shabbos dinner was put in a low oven on Friday afternoon 'erev Shabbos', and it was specially planned to cook slowly all night. Served up the next day, it had an inimitable succulent flavour that even nostalgia does not exaggerate.

There was no home oven big enough to hold the meals that my mother cooked for our large family, which now included a lodger. She also catered for several sons-in-law and numerous relations who kept dropping in for meals. So she arranged with Mrs Glick in another baker's shop to leave the huge pot of cholent brown potatoes and lockshen kugell-puddings overnight in her bakehouse.

On Saturday mornings the front door of our flat in the tenement remained open so that even a bell need not be pulled

70

on the Sabbath. I did not hear Mrs Crawford, our downstairs neighbour, coming into the kitchen. 'Good morning,' she said, all small grey and bustling with a face like a pink cherub. 'Good Shabbos, if you're a Jew,' I replied. Mrs Crawford laughed. 'Well, now. You know I'm not. But a very good Sabbath to you, mi wee lass.' She was already busy with paper and wood to kindle the fire.

'Are ye not going to the synagogue this morning, then?'

'Och yes,' I replied. 'But I'm a bit late. I let the boys go without me. Boys are more important in a shul anyway. But I'll still be in time for the sweeties. They give them away every Saturday as you go home.' Mrs Crawford shook her head at me, smiling. 'You're a great one for your sweeties, aren't ye?'

After she had lit the fire, I started to dress into my Shabbos best clothes. Ma came through from the bedroom. She had on her old dressing gown, which she wore once a week on Saturday mornings.

'Stat you, Mrs Crawfor'?' she said sleepily.

'It's yoursel', Mrs Cowan. Havin a wee lie-in, are ye?' enquired Mrs Crawford.

Ma sat down heavily on the rocking-chair by the fire. 'I'm kinda tired from the Friday's work. It's a lot, you know.'

'Aye, ye're a warrior, Mrs Cowan. We all say that about ye.' Mrs Crawford rose from the fireplace and stood looking down at my mother. 'But at least you've something to show for your work. Your children are well brought-up. So polite and all when we meet them on the stairs.'

I sniggered in the background. Ma threw me an angry look. 'Ach, yes,' she shook her fist at me, half smiling, 'some of them are. Some of them are.'

Her face became serious again. 'Still, mus'n' grumble,' Ma shrugged and went on. 'All the same. It's not good to be a widow without a man.'

'Oh aye,' replied Mrs Crawford. 'I'd agree with you there

in most cases. But not in my life. For I've got a man like a wobbly walking-stick. You cannae lean on him. Sometimes, you're better without one.'

Ma looked reflective. 'That's a good point. Maybe you got someting there.'

Mrs Crawford blew some life into the weakening flames of the fire. 'And,' she puffed a word with every breath, 'I wish my children were half as good as yours. Your people are all such tryers. I'll say that for ye. I mean, look at your girls. Do they still go to Rothesay even in the winter?'

Ma ran her hand across her brow. 'Ach, yes. That's our main business in Rothesay. Without that we couldn' make a living. And Largs and places like that. But it's very hard in the winter. Very rough on the boats on stormy days. I worry a lot.'

'Well, anyway,' said Mrs Crawford, rising again from her efforts at the fire, 'your family's a real credit to ye, Mrs Cowan.'

'Tank God! He's been good to me.'

Mrs Crawford pursued her point. 'Still, I think most Jews are hard workers.'

'I dunno,' Ma glared at her. 'Jews or not. We all gotta work.'

'Aye, ye're right there,' Mrs Crawford added hurriedly. Then, trying to placate my mother, Mrs Crawford went on, 'We're all going the same road, anyway. It's coming, aye it's coming, that man to man will brothers be for aa that. As Rabbie Burns says.'

'Oh!' said Ma, thinking this over. 'Did he say that? Rabbi Burns?' queried Ma. 'Well, I don't tink I know him. He doesn't belong to *my* synagogue.'

Turning as she reached the kitchen door, Mrs Crawford shouted, 'Well, now. There's your fire going a treat. I'll be back in the afternoon to stoke it up for you.'

'Tanks a lot, Mrs Crawfor'.'

'Ye're welcome, dear.' Mrs Crawford's voice echoed back.

Ma muttered to herself. 'Always the same. Always you gotta convince them that Jews are people, too.'

I shouted goodbye to my mother and skipped along the street, avoiding the cracks on the pavement, singing inwardly: '*Saturday! Saturday! Ess-ai-tee-yew-are-dee-ai-wy! Saturday.*' Then I made a run for the Talmud Torah Hebrew school and synagogue. As planned, I was just in time for the end of the service. Entering the back door of the synagogue I queued up with the other children as they were leaving at the front door. The guild lady at the doorway, quite unsuspecting, handed me my packet of sweets as I filed through.

Jacky, Wally, and I had our usual instructions to go straight to Mrs Glick's bakery and carry the big pot home in time for dinner. The door of the bakery was also left unlocked so that no-one need be on duty on Shabbos. We ran into the hot bakehouse. It was dark and steamy. The oven, at our waist level, ran deep and long, full of large pans hissing away.

'Here,' shouted Jacky. 'That one looks like ours. The old brown one with the dent in the lid.'

'That's it,' I said. 'Though it doesn't look big enough for our lot.' We found a long shovel-type pole and, inserting it under the pot, we pulled it towards us.

'Right, you two,' Jacky ordered. 'Get your gloves on. Hang on to these handles. And we'll get away down the road.'

We ran as fast as we could with the heavy, steaming utensil. Everything had still to be piping hot when we reached home. Puffing up the three flights of stairs, we rested our steaming burden on the doormat, then, with our last breath, rushed it into the kitchen. All the unmarried members of the family were already seated, waiting for their dinner.

Jacky, Wally, and I heaved the hissing pot on to the table. My sisters and brothers got their knives and forks ready. Ma quickly removed the lid. She screamed, 'This is not my pot! Look at that cholent full of barley and beans. That's not the way I make it. It belongs to some of them Polisher people.'

There was a great rivalry between the Litvaks and the Poles. They had a different kind of cooking and pronunciation of Yiddish. 'Ach, dear me,' Ma sighed. 'Never a doll moment. Those kids, you can't send them anywhere.'

'Well it's too late to change now,' remarked Jacky philosophically. 'Let's just eat and get it over with.'

Ma served dinner, and we all fiddled around with the unusual brand of cooking. In many years of ravenous family eating, this was the only meal I ever knew to be left on our hard-used kitchen table.

In the early part of Saturday afternoon, my brothers and myself hung around the closemouth. We waited patiently for Lily to come along and give us our Saturday pocket-money. At last she turned the corner of Apsley Place, stepping along trim and smart in a new hat. She noticed our sad faces right away. It was a little game we played with her. We knew she would give us the money. And she knew we knew we would get it. But we loved to play out our weekly act. 'Well,' Lily smiled perkily at us. 'Why all the sad faces?'

'Och, you know,' we jointly replied. 'No money for the pictures. It's nearly time to go.'

'And how much is it today?' she enquired.

'Well, we never collected any jam jars for pennies this week,' Jacky said. 'So we've really no money of our own to start us off. It would need to be sixpence each.' Lily was already delving into her purse. 'Heavens! You kids get more expensive every week. Here,' she laughed as she handed us the coins, 'sixpence each. Run away and enjoy yourselves. You're only young once.'

We ran like mad hares to join the noisy queue of shrieking children outside the Bedford Picture House. When we finally got in, we were just in time to find Pearl White hanging from the cliff where we had left her the previous

Saturday. At the end of the episode she was sinking in quicksand until next week.

It was barely light in the streets as we returned home. Our money had not stretched to chocolate bars. We were very hungry. Supper was always late on Saturday nights. Ma would do no cooking until the Holy Day ended. During the day all the Jewish shops were closed for Shabbos. But on Saturday night in the autumn, the old Gorbals came to life. As soon as dusk fell, the Sabbath day was officially over. Bearded men shuffled out of the synagogues after davenning their prayer 'Hav dolla.' Clinking the keys of their shops, they shouted greetings to each other as they opened the doors.

It was the best night of the week for business. Everywhere the darkness became lightened by gas mantles puttering alive to the new week. Blinds were drawn up. Bright lights began to shine from all the shop windows.

Out came the smelly shmaltz herring barrels. Out came the stalls displaying pickled cucumbers, smokies, and flatties, and, at bargain prices, the squashy tomatoes and mangy vegetables left over from Friday afternoon. Quickly set up were the racks of toys and fancy goods. Behind their meat-hung windows, blue-aproned butchers sharpened their carving knives in preparation for a busy evening. Rare new electric lights sparkled over Diamond's Dance Hall, ready for a big night.

As we climbed the three flights of stairs to our tenement home, the appetizing smell of baked tatties in their jackets and shmaltz herring wafted down to us. This was our traditional Saturday night supper. About eight o'clock that same Saturday evening in September Ma asked me to go out shopping with her. I looked round the kitchen. Jacky was compiling a home-made crossword puzzle, which Wally and I would try to solve the next day.

My big brother George (a tall, curly, handsome youth of twenty-one) and wee Wally were playing a duet on their violins. Even at the best of times the two violins sounded like a pair of sick cats let out for the night. It seemed worse than ever that night, because George was in the throes of the great love affair of his life. Soulfully, he tsooped away at the strings in his best *pizzicato* style. One more glance around the kitchen and I had no hesitation in agreeing to go out with her.

Ma had only recently acquired this desire for some of us to learn to play a musical instrument. Our family were already clinging to the lower rungs of the social ladder. My mother's cultural aspirations were praiseworthy enough. There was only one trouble. She had no discrimination in this matter.

Army style, she would say: 'You two! George-sonny and Walter. I fixed for you to learn the violin.' Then she went on: 'Katie, I paid for you to have piano lessons.'

There is no harm in a little parental compulsion. But my sister Kate will admit to this day that she is tone-deaf, that she cannot hum a popular piece of music even after it is played a hundred times on the radio.

Nevertheless, Ma was in her stubborn mood. Katie was chosen, and Katie had to go every week to the Athenaeum in the city of Glasgow to learn to play the piano. After a year or so at that highly respected institution, she could play 'The Rustle of Spring' quite well. Not by ear, but from sheer mechanical repetition.

George and Wally scraped away at their second-hand violins. And about that instrument, I think they liked best the dramatic gesture of throwing the little squares of velvet over their shoulders and bowing before they started.

The little green elf of envy lives inside all of us and often popped up in me. I wanted to take dancing lessons. But money for the arts had temporarily run out. Still, I sometimes visualized myself, flailing my imaginary long blue-veined arms across the stage in the death-scene from *Swan Lake,* a ballet that my sister Kate had taken me to see – my plump body as frail as any Degas ballet dancer's, and, the final curtain, the audience rising in tumultuous acclaim.

As Ma and I descended the circular staircase of the close, Annie and Rina were arriving home from their Saturday matinée in the Palace picture house in Main Street. They were giggling away as usual.

'Did you hear that man next to me?' Rina laughed. 'He offered me a sixpence just for a feel at my breast.' The two of them went into hysterics. Then Annie turned serious. 'I'm so glad we ran away from there. Ma always says don't speak to strange men. It's just as well we made a run for it.'

'Yes, that's all very well,' complained Rina. 'But we didn't see the picture through twice like we always do.' Luckily Ma's hearing was not as good as mine. We all met on the first landing.

'Here, you two!' shouted Ma. 'See and get your potatoes out of the oven. I'll soon be back with more herrings.'

I trotted along beside Ma down Apsley Place. Here and there men and women were ambling out from their closes after a Shabbos afternoon of sleep and lazing by the fire. Nearly everyone called greetings to us. 'A goot voch to you, Mrs Cowan.'

'And a bessern to you,' Ma replied. She gripped my hand as we crossed the now crowded tram-ridden thoroughfare. We stopped in at Glick's bakery. Ma explained to Mrs Glick about the mix-up of the pots in the morning. While they were commiserating with each other on the stupidity of children, I peeped into the bakehouse. It was now bright and busy. I noticed a long piece of ash dropping, from the cigarette hanging from Mr Glick's mouth, into the rolling dough. No matter, it would not stop the rush for baigles on Sunday morning. Ma's shopping-bag seemed full enough to me. But she kept going quite a distance. I was a bit fed up by this time.

So as to keep me quiet, she gave me a pickled cucumber

77

to suck. At last we came to a window hung with large sides of meat.

Our feet fluffed on sawdust as we entered the shop. Mr Vineberg the butcher greeted Ma rather coldly, I thought. And here I must explain about my mother's favourite hobby. In her spare time from cooking, baking, cleaning, mending, tending children and plants, wine-making, Passover grocery agent and credit draper, my mother was an amateur 'shadchan', a matchmaker, who brings people together with a view to marriage. So far she had not had any chance to use her latent talent on any of her own daughters, for the Jewish young men of the district were snatching my sisters off the family tree like ripe apples. But she had successfully matched up a few couples who were now living happily ever after.

Unhappily, to date, she had not had any luck with Mr Vineberg's slightly bearded daughter. He shook his head sadly. His spectacles slid down his long nose. 'Well, Mary. You promised me you'd have somebody else by now. You know how I'd like to get my Dora settled down and married. With her having no mother and all.'

'But that's what I came all this way just to tell you, Mr Vineberg,' said Ma. 'I got just the very young man. He's the son of a friend of mines from Edinburgh.'

Mr Vineberg wiped his nose with his blue-striped apron. 'And do you think it'll be aa-right for my Dora? Things did'n' go too well the last time we tried.'

Ma drew herself up haughtily. 'Can I help it if the young man don't like your daughter? I can't make them fall in love. I can only bring them together.'

The butcher looked downhearted. Ma tried to cheer him up. 'This time I deffinily tink it will be OK. Deffinily! I can feel it in mine bones. Beshert! Fated! Such a nice young Yiddisher boy. Edinburgh people are so refined, don't you tink?'

Mr Vineberg, the butcher, looked doubtful. 'I dunno. I never met anyone from that city.'

'Anyway,' went on my mother, full of enthusiasm, 'I gotta great idea. And I come special to tell you. You know my daughter Rae is getting married?' Ma never waited for an answer when she was excited. 'Well,' she went on, 'I'm inviting you and your daughter Dora to the wedding. At the same time this young man from Edinburgh. It's just the place for them to meet, natural-like.'

Suddenly the butcher's expression changed. He was bubbling over with delight. Not only was he getting a second chance to marry off his hirsute female offspring, but also an invitation to a wedding. He pulled a fierce-looking knife from the counter and yanked a side of meat out from the window. Cutting off a huge piece, he beamed at Ma. 'Ach, great! I mighta known you'd think of something, Mary. That's the best news I've heard today. Here, take this piece of runner.' He started to cut the meat. 'Make your family a nice tseemas for Sunday's dinner. No charge!'

Ma stuffed the parcel into her shopping bag. 'Tanks a lot,' she murmured. The butcher waved us off with his big knife. 'A good voch to you and yours.'

'And a bessern to you, Mr Vineberg,' Ma called back. 'I'm sure it will be. See you and Dora at the wedding.'

SUNDAY MORNING AT
GORBALS CROSS

Every Sunday morning, in the years that I remember, the shnorrers gathered at Gorbals Cross. As the crowds milled around, men hurried on their way with bags of baigles, coochons, and, 'if you were a rich man', smoked salmon for breakfast. Here and there a few women, who did not feel like lying late, made a quick round of the butchers' shops for Sunday dinner.

Gorbals Cross was not exactly a cross but more of a circle. Sentries of tall grey tenements cordoned it. Four roads converged on its centre, above which loomed a high standard lamp-post with a clock on it. Below this lay an oblong of spiked railings guarding the entrance to a much-used gents' underground lavatory.

While Glasgow and the rest of Scotland observed the now deceased strict Scottish Sabbath, the Gorbals was a teeming market of open shops, shouting people, and, of course, the congregating place of the shnorrers.

The chief of the shnorrers was a man everyone called Soap. No-one knew his real name. He was a big, grizzled, ruddy-faced man swathed in a long bulky overcoat, green with age, its pockets bulging with bars of soap and what appeared to be its owner's worldly possessions.

Soap, his pale blue eyes blinking above a slightly bulbous nose, was not slow to inform all and sundry that as a shnorrer he was a large cut above a beggar. Soap's attitude could make his victim believe that he really owed the old man the money, and that if the few coins were not forthcoming, in exchange for a bar of soap, something unpleasant would happen in the near future. Shnorring is a fine art. And Soap was a dedicated artist.

Evelyn's parents Simon and Mary Cowan circa 1908 with five daughters; one girl cousin and first-born son George in his father's arms.

(*Top*) In the 1880s: Evelyn's mother, Mary Banks (then unmarried), between her sisters, as they arrived from Lithuania into Scotland.

(*Bottom*) On the boat to Rothesay, Isle of Bute, summer 1930. *Left to right*: Evelyn (scarf hats were popular then!), Mother, brother Walter, niece Sylvia and sister Lily.

The entire family at a wedding of one of the sisters. Mother is in
the centre holding a grandchild. The married sisters are seated
(*second row*), with their husbands standing at the back. Brother
George is behind Mother; Evelyn is in the front row, second
from right.

(*Top*) The old South Portland Street Synagogue, 1924, the centre of social activities in Glasgow's Gorbals. It has been replaced by a block of high-rise flats.

(*Bottom*) Evelyn Cowan with her three grown-up sons, 1989. *Left to right*: Mark, Eric, Evelyn, and Jonathan.

He held court at Gorbals Cross, surrounded invariably by the smaller fry of his profession. On the fringe of the crowd gathered bookies, taking bets for Monday morning; muffered men escaping from female company for a while; and youths of the Gorbals out for a bit of Sunday morning fun.

My sister Annie and I were sent to buy baigles before going off to Hebrew Sunday School. As we had the curiosity of normal children, the crowd around the shnorrers always attracted us.

Soap was a born storyteller. Annie and I were regular listeners to his tales. He had a fund of stories which, I realized in later years, were strictly from Chelm. But every now and then he came up with a Soap original. On that Sunday morning he told one.

'Now,' said Soap, his rough yet quite angelic face beaming. 'I'm going to tell you the story of my life, and how I came to be a shnorrer.'

He spotted the familiar figures of my sister and me on the outskirts of the crowd and waved us forward.

'Let the little girls in, I want them to hear better. I love wee Yiddisher lassies.'

My sister Annie and I pushed through to the front. Our arms round each other's girlish waists, we stood gazing up at Soap. Annie's serious adolescent eyes and my trusting eight-year-old face looked at him expectantly.

'As a matter of fact,' the shnorrer seemed to be addressing himself specially to us, 'it's because of my liking for girls – all kinds of girls – that I finally came to be standing here like this.'

Soap pointed to his bulky body and prickly chin. He had a large vocabulary, a smooth resonant voice with hardly a trace of the broken English accent such as we were accustomed to in the first generation of Eastern-European-Scottish immigrants.

'You know,' went on Soap. 'I never came from the old country like your people.' He wagged his grubby finger at Annie and me. 'I come from a long line of real Scots Highland folk. Would you believe that?'

We shook our childish heads in disbelief. 'Yes, I come from the lochs, the glens, the hills, and the beautiful countryside around Loch Lomond. And,' Soap continued in an imitation sing-song Highland tone, 'at the time of the 'Forty-Five my forefathers were henchmen of Bonnie Prince Charlie.'

The crowd stood spellbound now. Soap held sway. 'My real name is Ian MacFinkelstein, and I was born in a clachan not far from the famous clachan of Aberfoyle.

'Yess,' Soap was quite carried away with his Highland Scottish accent. 'In 1746, when Prince Charles was defeated at Culloden, my ancestor Douglas MacFinkelstein formed one of the small loyal bunch who, aided by Flora Mac-Donald, helped our Bonnie Prince to escape to the Isle of Skye *en route* for France. My ancestor, the Douglas of Douglas, was one of the last persons to be with our sad, dear Prince before he stepped from his native soil.'

For a moment there was silence while the shnorrer allowed the tale to sink into the minds of his audience. Then old Soap reached into a capacious pocket of his shabby coat. He brought out a package, unwrapped its mottled sticky paper, and produced a bar of soap. Without a murmur from the assembly close around him, he went on – 'Observe, Ladies and Gentlemen, this Object.'

Soap held the smelly bar aloft for all to see. 'This is no ordinary piece of soap. This is the very bar of soap, yes, the very one, that the hands of our dear Prince Charlie touched just before he went into exile. And all I'm asking for it, my good people, is one shilling. One shilling! For a treasure of Scottish history. Why! It may be worth thousands of pounds in an antique shop in Edinburgh today!'

'Here is your chance,' Soap continued, his voice rising. 'It may be that you will make a fortune. And if not,' the shnorrer grinned cheekily, 'if not, well at least you will have some soap to wash your hands clean.'

'Rubbish!' came a voice. A prosperous looking man at the back of the crowd repeated, 'Rubbish! It's just plain carbolic soap. You can buy it for twopence a bar in any shop.'

The pale blue eyes of the shnorrer assumed an injured look. 'Sir,' he beckoned the well-dressed man. 'Come forward.' The heckler edged his way to the front of the crowd. The chief of the Gorbals shnorrers held the large bar of soap to the man's nose.

'Does that smell like an ordinary bar of soap which you could buy every day in a shop? This soap is almost two hundred years old.'

The man sniffed. 'Aye. It certainly smells like it.'

Sadly Soap withdrew the bar and made to put it back in his pocket, saying gruffly, 'No good will come to you this year, my man. You have doubted the word of a descendant of the Douglas of Douglas. And brought bad luck on your family for a mere shilling.'

The man hurriedly dug a silver coin from his jacket pocket, pushed it into Soap's outstretched hand, and walked quickly away through the crowd.

'Who else would doubt the word of Ian MacFinkelstein?' The shnorrer walked around the people with his palm turned upwards. Nearly everyone put a few coppers in it. 'But, Soap,' I piped bravely, 'you were going to tell us how you came to be a shnorrer.'

A youth at the back shouted, 'And from such high-born people, too!' The grizzled old man had collected a few shillings. He returned to centre stage of his pavement theatre.

'Oh, yes, lass.' He patted the top of my head benevolently. 'I was just coming to that.' Soap removed his greasy brown floppy hat and scratched his head for a moment. 'Yes,' he said slowly. 'Yes.'

Then suddenly he remembered his Highland Scots accent. 'It was thae English. That's it.' The shnorrer went on happily, 'The English. They hounded my ancestor, knowing that he had helped a pretender to the throne. So, through two

83

centuries the Clan MacFinkelstein went down and down in its fortunes. No trade, no profession remained open to us. Until at last, I find myself the only son of this generation – the last of the MacFinkelsteins, wandering through the towns and villages of Scotland.'

The old man seemed relieved that he had managed to reach the end of his story. 'But what about the lassies?' I persisted. The mind of a child wanted all the ends tied up. 'You said the lassies brought you to this.'

'Oh, yes.' Soap looked reflectively down at me. 'You have a good memory, wee girl,' he said sadly. 'Better than mine.' He murmured out of the side of his mouth. 'How many Sundays have you been coming here?' Soap enquired.

'I come quite a lot,' I replied.

'Have you heard all my stories, then?'

'No: I miss a few sometimes when I sleep in and I'm running late for chader.' The shnorrer sighed with relief, obviously trying to steer away from my questions. He shouted, 'Chader! What's chader?' A sharp blonde Jewish housewife stepped forward. 'Come off it, Soap,' she shrieked. 'You know what a Hebrew school is. You're Yiddish. I've seen you in the synagogue.'

Old Soap seemed glad of the diversion. 'I do not deny that I am a Jew. But on the other hand, madam, you cannot refute my claim that my ancestors were at Culloden in 1746.'

'I'm sure!' the sharp woman shrilled sarcastically. 'But, for your information, there were no Jews in Scotland two hundred years ago.' Soap looked at her with wounded pride. 'Madam, you are wrong. And if you will return here next Sunday morning and purchase from me one bar of soap, I will produce for you the documents proving my ancestry. Written proof, Madam.' Without answering immediately, the housewife came forward shaking her fist. 'All right, well,' she shouted at Soap. 'So what about the lassies, Mr MacClever? Finish your story, if you can.'

I had taken a dislike to the sharp woman. My childish heart surged towards Soap. I prayed that he would not fail.

'The lassies, eh, well . . .' Soap cleared his throat. His eyes lit up. Then quickly he went on. 'Yes, well . . . I've loved all kinds of girls in my lifetime. But the one I loved the most was my own sister Flora.'

The old shnorrer was off again, and I felt glad. He pointed to my sister Annie, whose straight fringed dark hair and deep blue eyes made her look more like a flower of Highland nobility than a poor child of a Jewish family standing at Gorbals Cross that Sunday morning.

'My sister Flora was almost as beautiful as this lass over here. Yes, beautiful,' Soap went on. 'She was called Flora after Flora MacDonald who cherished Bonnie Prince Charlie and helped him to escape. But my Flora did not have such a good life. Many years ago she met and married a no-good scoundrel. An Irish-Jewish bastard, if ever there was one.'

Waving his floppy hat, Soap bowed to the blonde lady, 'If you will excuse the language, ma'am.' Whether he realized it or not, the shnorrer now spoke in a thick Irish brogue. He continued, 'His name was Patrick Michael Dunnovitch. The day she married him was the sorriest day of her life. If only my sister had known it. That Irish wretch, that drunken sod left her to starve and die with her newborn bairn in her arms.'

My sister Annie and I had our little hankies out.

But the sharp woman interposed, 'And where do you come into this, Soap?' He dismissed her. 'Don't be so impatient, Missis. I'm coming to that. Naturally, I helped my beloved sister whenever I could. In fact, I poured my money and all my worldly goods on her until the day she died. Then, having buried my own Flora, I found myself without means or occupation. I took to the roads, tramping around the byways of Scotland and became, by profession, a shnorrer.'

The old man really had the story spinning now. 'But

Nemesis, the Goddess of Retribution, never fails to serve the righteous and the just.'

Soap smiled kindly down at me as if to assure me that everything was going to be all right in the end. 'So, one summer's day, when I was shnorring along the seafront at Largs, I spotted him. Yes, himself, Patrick Michael Dunnovitch. The scoundrel, the digger of the grave of my sister Flora and her babe.'

Annie and I were weeping copiously now. Soap went on. 'There Patrick walked in the sun, looking handsome and healthy. I edged along the promenade, weaving my way in and out between the gaming machines and the weighing machines, making myself ready to catch him and do him a mortal injury – when surely he must have realized he was being followed. He started to run. Pushing through the crowds of people, past the ice-cream-vendors, then round the benches facing the sea.'

Jumping with excitement, we children were hanging on every word. 'And at last you caught him, eh Soap?' my sister said breathlessly. 'Na lass, na.' Soap buttoned up his long dirty overcoat, preparing to depart. 'You see, after all that chase, I was as close to him as I am to you now. And what do you think happened to cheat me of my rightful revenge?' My sister and I shook our heads, not knowing the answer. 'I'll tell you,' beamed Soap, making a path for himself through the crowd. 'I'll tell you. He, that Patrick Michael Dunnovitch, he jumped on one of them weighing-machines and got a-weigh.'

Soap the Shnorrer strode smartly into a lane off Main Street, Gorbals. His retreating figure resembled a distant outline of Ben Lomond. 'Got away! Got *AWAY*!' We could hear his rich thespian voice echoing down the lane and through the myriad of little streets which ran, like veins, through the Gorbals.

When I think of Soap's story now, a twinkle comes into my eyes. 'Got a-weigh.' It was one of the oldest Glasgow music hall jokes. I'd heard it dozens of times at the Princess Theatre in Main Street. But it was not until many years later that I heard the real ending to Soap the shnorrer's story.

I was spending a few days in a seaside hotel in Largs (funnily enough). There I met an old school friend, Sam Kaufman. We got to talking about the good old days when we munched our baigles and listened to Soap's stories on Sunday mornings at Gorbals Cross. It was then that Sam Kaufman began to tell me the incredible story of Soap's true identity.

My childhood friend, Sam Kaufman, had been for many years a voluntary official of the Glasgow Hebrew Burial Society. One of his jobs was to see to the proper religious burial of Jewish paupers in the city. One day, Sam was called to a sleazy hostel building in the East End of Glasgow, a hostel noted for its intake of tramps, alcoholics, and general layabouts.

Sam was shown up three flights of stairs. He entered the filthy, almost bare room. And, sure enough, the body on the bed was unmistakably old Soap the Shnorrer, lying dead in the bulgy green overcoat, with the same pleasant, beaming smile on his face as in life.

After closing Soap's eyes, Sam covered him with a ragged grey blanket. Then he started going through the carpet-bag lying open on the floor. It was doubtful, Sam told me, if there had been any money. But even a few coppers would have been removed by the inhabitants of the hostel long before Sam got there.

Obviously, Sam said, the bag had been searched. A black leather cloth lay unwrapped, and some papers were lying loose nearby. Picking up the bundle, Sam leafed through the papers, which turned out to be Soap's birth certificate, old family snapshots and a letter to be opened in the event of the shnorrer's death.

My friend Kaufman explained that there was no doubt about Soap's identity. He had come from one of the first arrivals of Jewish families to Scotland. The death certificates showed that the parents had died soon after arrival. And their two sons, according to some press cuttings, had gone on to found two of the wealthiest families in the Jewish community of Glasgow.

There were snapshots of Soap in his young days, handsome, nicely dressed, and still beaming. The resemblance to his brother was quite remarkable. Then came document after document showing his long legal wrangles with his brother through the courts claiming his share in the family business. Some more snaps of Soap in various theatrical costumes clipped to old programmes of obscure theatres in little seaside towns along the Ayrshire coast.

Later, in his office at the Hebrew Burial Society, Rutherglen Road, Gorbals, Sam Kaufman opened the letter taken from Soap's bundle of documents. It was a long recounting of the business squabbles of the two brothers and Soap's final defeat in court. The end of the letter was a vivid description of the Shnorrer's lonely life tramping around the countryside in the West of Scotland.

In the final paragraph Soap wrote: 'In death I feel no bitterness. Tell my brother Bernard, I forgive him. Better we should meet again at seemchas and parties. I wish him long life.'

The address of the brother, who was next of kin, was stated on the document. And Sam Kaufman told me he put it in a fresh envelope and addressed it as directed. Sam wrote on the envelope:

Sir Bernard Nevilsky,
Lord Provost of Glasgow,
City Chambers,
George Square,
Glasgow, Scotland.

A WEDDING

Our big kitchen in the tenement apartment in Apsley Place, Gorbals, was a hive of activity. Over by the window, my sister Tilly pedalled away on a borrowed sewing machine. Littered on the floor were coloured threads, bits of white satin, mauve tulle and yellow silk. My sister Rose sat by the fire hand-stitching a dress.

Wedding preparations were in full swing, for it was only a few days before the great day. The bridal train was rapidly approaching panic stations. Ma kneeled down on the floor and pulled my long purple silk dress into shape. I fidgeted restlessly. Ma looked up at me. 'Will she ever make a girl, do you think? Mine tomboy footballer, eh?'

Sometimes I wondered. My friend Rosie Schulberg told me she had read an almanack which said that a girl could change into a boy if she prayed to the moon in a certain way every night. But the girl would require to be under thirteen. I had a few years yet. So Rosie Schulberg and I went down into the back yard every night, faced the moon, and prayed earnestly. Boys were more fun than girls, anyway. And I prayed especially hard. But so far my prayers had not been answered.

On this evening my desire for boyhood began to fade. I experienced, for the first time, faint stirrings of feminine interest in a dress. The boys were in dress rehearsal of navy blue serge suits and white shirts. For once I did not envy them. I felt quite pretty in my bridesmaid's dress. My sister Rose came over to me and started to mark places for sewing on the yellow rosebuds.

The bride-to-be had not arrived home from Rothesay. But the future bridegroom came up into the kitchen to join in the fun and give his approval to the colour scheme. Louis was

89

a tall, angular, jutting-jawed sort of chap. Quite the most handsome man I had seen since my first acquaintance in celluloid with Ricardo Cortez. But Louis was not so dark-haired as he. At a glance from my new brother-in-law to be, I could be tempted away from my idol.

However, Louis's attitude to me was not conducive to romance. He liked to lift me in the air and swing me around like a merry-go-round. I felt quite giddy, for two reasons. My mother never could pronounce his name. She called him 'Loo-yee'. He was a barber by trade and had been to college to learn about shapes of heads and bone structure. He had wanted to be a doctor. And his parents were in a good enough position, financially, to help him study. But they lived in a slightly lower-class street than Apsley Place.

Even our little ghetto had its fine social distinctions. Where we had a bathroom with a real bath inside our house, Louis's family shared a common stair-head lavatory with three other families. Louis's mother was afraid the neighbours would think her very uppish at having ambitions of sending her son to study medicine at Glasgow University. After all, Louis was already stepping up socially, marrying into a family who had a bathroom in the house. And Louis's mother did not want the neighbours to be jealous – about his being a doctor, not about his marrying into a family with a bathroom. So she only allowed him to go to barber school. However, Rae and Louis lived to see their son become a famous bone surgeon in California and have much pleasure from his good work.

Rae had no appetite for the meal that Ma put out. Hands clasped, the lovers sat on the edge of the curtained recess bed, quite indifferent to the chaos of the kitchen. Ma seemed quite content with this, provided she could see their legs dangling over the side. She turned a blind eye to their quick stolen kisses.

The front door remained open, despite a cold autumn draught. There was no point in closing it, because friends and neighbours kept dropping in with wedding presents.

Each new female arrival had to have a quick preview of the bridal gown and going-away outfit. During the evening, there was an uproar in the lobby. Mrs Schulberg and Mrs Kaplan were on their way out. They had bumped into Mrs Solomons, a friend of Ma's, who was just entering. There were sounds of altercations between the three women. At last Mrs Solomons, a dark, sallow, eastern-looking woman, crashed into the kitchen. She rushed up to Ma and, folding her arms belligerently, confronted my mother.

'I heard you invited the rest of them with their families.' Mrs Solomons jerked her head indicating the departing neighbours. 'So why wasn't my son Moishe invited, eh?' She rattled on. 'Don't you think I would like him to meet some nice Yiddisher girls instead of running around the town with sheiksas, eh?'

Ma was quite taken aback. 'But there must be some mistake, Mrs Solomons. My daughter Rosie did all the writing. She has such a neat hand. I tot it was all checked up.' Mrs Solomons weakened visibly. 'Do you mean you invited my Moishe?'

'Well, I'm sure of it. Your family was on the list . . . Just tell Moishe to come. There's no time to send more invitations, anyway.'

'Oy thank you, Mrs Cowan.' Mrs Solomons seemed so happy. 'You're a lady. I knew you would'n' do such a thing to an old friend.'

She departed in peace. After she left, my sister Rose went to Ma. Rose said quietly, 'Ma. You know that Moishe Solomons was not invited.' Ma shrugged. 'So? Anything for a quiet life. Just now everyone's my best friend. I never had so many friends before. And I don't want any more freebles. I got plenty.'

The last few days before the wedding passed in a gathering momentum of excitement. One dress was too long. Another was too short. Most of us younger children slept well, despite the night-long hum of voices and sewing machines.

Early on the morning of the wedding, Ma wakened us. We were all hair-washed and bathed, then left to sit around naked but enshrouded in large white sheets. Ma then escorted the bride to the Mikvah, the kosher ritual baths, where poor Rae was dunked in some kind of holy water, and then had a special blessing chanted over her by an official who waited behind a curtain in the baths.

The wedding ceremony was timed to start at 3.30 p.m. The bridal party were to proceed down the stairway of the close at 33 Apsley Place at three o'clock and parade along the street and round to the South Portland Street Synagogue. At two o'clock sharp, my mother blew a blast on a large whistle, borrowed from Jacky's Scoutmaster. This was the signal for all my sisters and brothers to assemble in the front room. The bride was then allowed to dress in Ma's bedroom.

My sister Rae, many weddings ago, had devised a marvellous method for getting a large family of children out to a wedding with a minimum of panicking over lost clothes and best socks and shoes. So on the previous night, the bride herself had placed round the huge polished oak table, every article of clothing which we would require the next day. Little, neat piles of clothes were bunched round the table. Each place had a ticket marked with a child's name. On top of the table lay vests, pants, dresses, hair ribbons, or shirts and suits pressed and folded nicely. Below each place, on the floor, was the appropriate pair of black patent shoes and white silk socks. We all marched into the room and round the table facing our own place name.

Ma had dressed earlier. To me, she looked lovelier than the bride. Her brown hair seemed lit with waves of white, her glasses had such pale rims that you scarcely noticed them, and her complexion was still so smooth that it did not seem to have been furrowed by years of hardship.

She had on a long black dress with white *broderie anglaise* collar and cuffs, my sister Tilly's patient handwork. As I gazed up at Ma's elegant throat, I could see she wore that same cameo brooch, her only keepsake from her own mother. Ma gave another blast on the whistle. We proceeded to dress in the clothes opposite us. Not one ribbon or shoe went missing. There was no commotion. By the time my sister Rae tumbled, starry-eyed, radiant but still our happy-go-lucky Rae, from the bedroom, we were all ready and dressed to fall in behind her to the synagogue.

The ladies of the Gorbals had turned out to see the wedding. There was a murmur of sighs as we came out into the street. All the young girls swayed dreamy-eyed, and the older women nodded their heads in unison as they held their hankies at the ready.

Very few of my friends recognized me stripped of my old football jersey and making my début as a bridesmaid. One or two fellow footballers looked me over in astonishment. 'Get a keek at her!' They nudged one another. Raising my shy eyes, I caught those of my friend Rosie Schulberg. I think she knew there would be no more prayers to the moon.

My mother always undertook the part of the father-of-the bride. Leaning on Ma's arm, Rae slow-stepped up the aisle to stand under the wedding canopy set up inside the Shul. Louis and his parents were already waiting under the chuppah.

The Rabbi, in his white robes and white velvet octagonal-shaped hat, stepped forward. He unfolded the parchment scrolled with ancient Hebrew letters. His assistant intoned the blessings. Then the couple were married according to the law of Moses and of Israel. Rae sipped the special wine from a silver beaker held by the best maid. Louis then crashed his foot down on a tumbler wrapped in brown paper to symbolize the bitterness of the Fall of the Temple in olden times.

Tears were streaming down my mother's face all through the ceremony. She was a lone figure – as always, playing both mother and father to her family.

Next door in the synagogue hall, friends, and relations set out the prepared food and wine. The musicians tuned up their instruments. All happy and gay now, the wedding party arrived to start dancing. 'Mazeltov! Mazeltov!' everyone shouted. The bridal couple were first to waltz away. Then Jacky asked me to dance. We had been practising for weeks. The reason why he danced with me all evening was that only he and I knew the steps he had invented. Smug at all the admiring glances, we danced along. Little did they know he was barking in my ear, 'One, two, three. Ouch! that's my toe. One, two, three, you big heavy lump! Four, five, six, lift your feet, for God's sake!'

All my family danced past. There were Tilly, Rose, and Lily with their husbands. George and his sweetheart danced by. Ma floated past in the arms of ginger-haired Mr Hornstein, Senior. Young Moishe Solomons dutifully waltzed by with one of the Schulberg girls.

During the evening, the rest of my sisters charlestoned with their latest boyfriends. And there was Dora Vineberg stepping it out with the young man from Edinburgh. Their meeting had been a big success, possibly because his short-sighted, blinking eyes only reached the tips of her breasts. His gaze never reached her hairy chin. For him, the future stood out prominently and happily.

Mr Vineberg the butcher and Mrs Solomons sat that dance out, their long noses slicing the air in merry unison to the rhythm of the music. Beside them at the table sat fair-haired Mr and Mrs Tenter. They were Ma's posh friends from the far end of Apsley Place. Ma had invited them to lend prestige to the whole affair. For Mr Tenter was not an Eastern European Jew like the rest of our neighbours. He was a blond Jewish diamond merchant from Antwerp. Mrs Tenter had a little maid to help in the house. They possessed a telephone, the only one in the entire street.

Soon it was time for the honeymoon couple to leave. We all trooped out on to the pavement. Rae emerged dressed up in her short tight costume and maribou-feathered hat – not to be outdone by Louis, who was resplendent in double-breasted grey pinstripe suit, grey spats, and large grey Windsor tie, with huge Homburg hat to match.

Tears were the order of the parting all round. Rae clung to Ma until the last minute. The honeymoon was to be spent in Troon, a little seaside town about twenty-five miles along the Ayrshire coast road from Glasgow. Ma comforted the bride.

'It'll be so lovely at this time of the year by the sea. Don't catch cold. Take care of yourself, my daughter.' Rae was too overcome to speak. Louis put his arm around his bride and drew her gently away. Most of the family and guests returned to the hall. Ma and I waved from the pavement's edge until the cab rounded the corner en route for Waterloo Street bus station.

Ma was crying quietly into her lace hankie. We remained there standing together, two forlorn remnants of the wedding. I reached up and gripped Ma's hand. I wanted her to know that she was not alone, that there were still some of us left. Squeezing my hand in reply, Ma cleared her throat and looked down at me. 'Noo?' she said. 'One day it will be your turn. Then my job will really be done.'

Two days later we were still tidying the house of papers and strings and confetti, when a very unusual thing happened.

The front door bell rang. I answered the ring. It was Ida Tenter, the only child of the well-off family down the street. 'Hullo there,' I said diffidently. I always had a guilty feeling about Ida. She was a nice girl and always wanted to be friends. But it seemed like too much trouble to go for her and wait until the maid called her to the door, when I could easily shout up from the middle of the street to my friend, 'Hey Rosie, come'n out to play!'

However on that day, Ida gasped breathlessly, 'Tell your mother to come quickly. She's wanted on the telephone.'

'The what?' I screamed.

'Hurry up! The telephone. It's a special trunk call.' I ran

into the kitchen and delivered this astounding message to Ma. She looked extremely startled. And without waiting to put on our coats, we raced down the street. Ma's slippers flapped up and down. Ida Tenter ran behind informing all passers-by of the important call.

At the foot of the street we ran up to the first-floor flat of the Tenters. Mrs Tenter already had the door open. Proudly, she played her role of the Duchess of Apsley, and showed Ma into her well-furnished hall. 'Come quick, Mrs Cowan,' she said haughtily.

'Oh, tanks, Mrs Tenter. Sorry troublin you. This is terrible. I wonder what it can be?'

Ma lifted the long earpiece. I jumped up on a chair and put my ear alongside. 'Ma,' I heard a plaintive voice. 'It's me, Rae.'

'Stat you, Rae? My goo'ness! What's the matter? Is anything wrong?'

'No, no,' said Rae hurriedly. 'Don't worry, I'm fine.'

'Then for why are you wasting money speaking on telephones?'

'Och, it's only money,' said my sister Rae in her life-long philosophy. 'I didn't mean to worry you. I'm really fine. But it's so far away here. Just the two of us. I miss you all so much. You and the girls and the kids.'

'Och, my! What a fright you give me!' Ma sighed with relief.

'Listen, Ma.' I could hear Rae crying. 'I want to come home please. Can I come home and spend the rest of my honeymoon with you and the family?'

And she did, too.

STREET GAMES

In the 1929-30s era, the Jewish people who lived in the Gorbals of Glasgow were a tight little community. Very few of us lived outside that district. We had our synagogues, our own meeting places, dance halls, and especially our own type of food shops. Congregating exclusively with our own kind, we hardly knew any Christian people.

But in the early 1930s the drift began. And thirty years before its physical destruction, the soul of the old Gorbals was flitting southwards towards suburbia. Small splinter communities sprang up everywhere. After losing its branches the old parochial tree gradually shrivelled up.

Now the Gorbals has gone. The Jewish people have gone. There is no need to shop in one particular district. Young housewives no longer have any desire to serve only kosher food. The supermarkets carry stocks of everything. Today, in what remains of the tenements, Pakistani families are living a life similar to what we once knew. I wonder if their grown-up children will suffer the pangs of acute nostalgia some day, too.

My Jewish people, as they bettered themselves, money-wise, did not want to live the narrow life of a ghetto. Scattering around Glasgow went the once poor, now middle-class shopkeepers. And, further away from them, the Jewish merchants prospered into wealthy citizens.

Somehow, I cannot imagine our sophisticated children of modern times, playing out in the street the simple mischievous games that we invented.

For, back in 1929, one dark afternoon in winter, my brothers, myself, and our gang were holding an initiation meeting for the new boy of the street. Harold had not long moved into Apsley Place. He had wanted all along to join our crowd.

So my brother Jacky-the-Jumbo arranged for us to meet in a close a few yards down the street from our home.

About eight of us were jammed into the musty narrow back close. There was Jacky, Wally and myself the only girl, not quite converted to full-time femininity. The crowd included Harold, a blankfaced pale boy of about ten. Big Doddy Hertsfield, a dod of a boy in a man's body, Ginger-Snotty Hornstein, Julie the Jewel, a flashy boy, and Peeshy-Paishy, a boy of thirteen with a heavy growth of hair on his face.

'Now, listen carefully.' Jacky addressed himself to Harold. 'This is part of your test to join our gang.'

'Aa right. I'm listening.' Harold became paler.

'Well,' Jacky went on, while the rest of us stood around in silence. 'You go up to the top of this building. Count up to fifty by fives. Then come jumping slowly down the stairs singing out loud, "It was me! It was me!"'

'You mean,' interrupted Harold, 'that's all I need to do?'

'Yes,' nodded Jacky, 'for the moment, anyway. Just do what you're told. And whatever happens, don't stop singing.'

Jacky gave the new boy a violent shove. 'Right, now! Away you go up.' Harold climbed the three flights of strange stairs. When he had gone, we all tiptoed up to the second storey. We tied a long string across the landing from the door handle of one flat to the bell-pull of the other. Working quickly, we did the same on the first floor.

Then I ran up and rapped at the door with the tied handle. I did the same on the landing below. I then disappeared down into the dark back close where the boys were waiting.

Meanwhile, the first lady opened her door, and in doing so, pulled her neighbour's door-bell. By this time, Harold was on his innocent descent, singing at the top of his voice, 'It was me! It was me!'

The two irate women caught hold of him. 'Oh, it was, was it? Can't you find anything better to do than ringing folk's bells?'

Harold received a good few slaps on his face. Then he continued down on to the first floor, where the two neighbours there grabbed him and boxed his ears. He was crying, but still bravely singing, 'It was me! It was me!' – and was a fully-fledged member of our gang as he joined us in jumping over the dyke to escape.

We raced along the lane beside Motherwell's flour mills and turned across the tramlines towards Oatlands. This was a district forbidden to us, notorious as it was for gangs. We mooched alongside the dim shop windows. There were no kosher butcher shops here. But mainly cut-price bacon, ham, and egg shops, and dusty windows displaying pails and ropes and sticky notebooks with erasers to match. Then we turned off into a side-street. Jacky called us to halt, we were far away from the noisy tram-clanging street. There was dead silence. Suddenly in the distance we heard the cry, 'Here come the Billy Boys!'

'It's the gangs,' shrilled Harold. 'We better get out of here quick.' In a flurry of excitement, we started to run for our own district. My heart thumped like a war drum. This was not the first time we had been chased by gangs. We spoke of them in whispered awe. Yet we were never caught.

And, strangely but truthfully, in all the years that I lived my childhood in the Gorbals of Glasgow, I never saw a gang-fight or a razor wielded in an attack.

We raced back across the tracks, turned into Apsley Place, ran through the first close and huddled together in the darkness. The noises of running feet could be heard passing by and voices shouting, 'A Billy or a Dan, or an old tin can!'

A Billy was a Protestant and a Dan was a Catholic. And an old tin can was a Jew. So if you admitted you were an old tin can, you got kicked around the street just like that piece of metal. Vaguely, we always knew of someone who got beaten up by the gangs. But it was never one of our immediate circle. Still, we shivered thrills of anticipation and the real dangers never quite penetrated our minds.

When the 'all clear' signal came from Julie, our temporary lookout, we formed a circle round the lamp-post on the pavement to decide what to do for the rest of the evening. A motley assortment of shapes and sizes we were. From Big Doddy round to Jumbo-Jacky, pale Harold, wee Wally, Skinny Julie, Snotty Hornstein, and ending with my small female self enveloped in a ragged cast-off football jersey.

Big Doddy said, 'Let's go down to the river under the bridge and see the wind blowing up the lassies' skirts?'

'Na,' said Julie. 'That wouldn't take up much time,' I interrupted. 'Anyway, that's no interest to me.'

'Aye. I forgot about you being a girl.' Doddy shuffled his feet.

'You've only forgot since my brother Jumbo punched you up OK.' Doddy fidgeted. 'Well, how about a smoke?'

'Haven't the price of it.' Wee Wally looked up at six-footer Doddy. 'Anyway, it'll stunt your growth.'

'Och, never mind all that,' Ginger Hornstein sniffed. 'How about a game of football?'

'It's too dark. You'd never be able to see the ball.' Jacky recovered his authority. 'That reminds me. What about Miss Duncan? We're about due a visit there.'

By a majority, we voted to have our revenge on Miss Duncan. Now, she was a lady who lived down our street in a main door flat. She had a beautiful patch of garden on each side of her front door, which faced the street. The gardens were guarded by medium-high spiked railings. Inevitably, when we played a game in the street, our ball went into Miss Duncan's well-kept garden. She must have been waiting at the ready. For the minute the ball touched her ground, she dashed out through her little side gate, into her garden, snatched the ball and in front of our very eyes cut up the ball with big scissors.

Our pleas and cries fell on deaf ears. She just kept on cutting. Tales were told in the street that Miss Duncan was more than one person, and that, supposedly, there were two

100

Miss Duncans. But this was never proved. They were both tall, wore long black tunic coats, and kept their grey hair drawn back in a tight bun.

One of them appeared to be slightly fatter than the other. But this may have been the one and only Miss Duncan after a big dinner. We were never sure. Her appearances in public were rare and swift. The other story about Miss Duncan was that she had been jilted on her wedding day by Paleface the Polisman. And that's why they always exchanged angry glances and both hated children.

It was usually afternoon, after school, when all our games were played. But by now it was evening. In pairs we drifted through the close into the yard at the back of Miss Duncan's flat. We threaded a safety-pin on a reel of black thread, fastened one end of the thread to a knob outside the spinster's window, reeled out the thread and span it along until we were far away. Then we let the pin slide down the thread until it tapped on the window.

'Tap . . . tap . . .' went the metal pin on the windowpane. Miss Duncan opened her window and put her head out. Quickly we tilted the thread downwards, leading the pin back to us. Seeing nothing, she withdrew and closed the window. We were round the corner in the darkness of the back yard.

As soon as she closed the window, we let the pin slide back on to the pane. 'Tap . . . tap . . .' Miss Duncan's head emerged again. There appeared to be nobody there. We repeated this for about an hour until Miss Duncan was nearly demented.

'Hey, you kids! Hooligans! I know you're out there,' she shouted into the darkness.

We giggled. She went on shouting. 'You just try it once more. And I'll call the police.' Wally yelled back at her, 'Pay us back for the balls?'

'Throw us out the money,' shouted Jacky.

Far away we could hear Ma's stentorian voice resounding

along the street. She was leaning dangerously out of our high window – 'Jacky, Wally, Ebby! . . . Nine o'clock!' It was time to go home. We trailed up our three flights of stairs. In the kitchen my sisters had steaming cups of hot cocoa and bread and jam prepared. We washed our hands. And while we sipped our nightly beverage, we enjoyed watching Annie and Rina play their kind of games. My sister Kate sat in a corner by the fire engrossed in her library book.

Annie and Rina were dressed up like ladies in Ma's old gowns with high-heeled shoes and big floppy picture hats. They had attached a rope to an old flatiron. This was their imaginary poodle. So now they were two smart society ladies out shopping and meeting for a chat. Annie tugged at her rusty iron poodle. 'Good morning. Miss Florence Nightingale, is it?' This greeting pleased Rina, for her ambition was to be a nurse. She had been diverted by Ma from choosing this occupation because Ma thought it was not a suitable job for a nice Jewish girl. However, Rina eventually made it into the nursing profession, although she was a grandma before she passed her final exam.

Back in the kitchen, Rina replied to Annie, 'Oh, yes. That's me. Pleased to meet you.' The two girl-ladies shook hands. 'And what's *your* name, my dear?' Rina waved her broken umbrella-cum-parasol. 'Oh, don't you remember me?' Annie simpered. 'We met at the Royal garden party in London. My name is Mrs Marjorie Seldon.'

The girls played out their gossipy act. But Annie's choice of Seldon as a name was not purely imaginary. For my father's real name had been Simon Zeldon. According to his traditional story, when his ship docked about the year 1900, Papa disembarked at Greenock. With hundreds of other refugees he queued up in the landing shed. Eventually he reached the desk of the immigration official. The busy officer looked over my father's papers. 'Your papers are in order.' He fingered the document. 'But I can't make out your name. What is it?'

My father, with only a few words of English at his command, could not comprehend the man. 'I said,' the officer was getting impatient, 'what is this name? How do you spell it?'

Papa Zeldon shook his head, pointing to his lips and then to the identity book, indicating his lack of language. 'Och, what's the odds?' The man was already wielding his rubber stamp, 'Let's call you Cohen like the rest of them.'

He wrote 'Cohen' across the illegible foreign words, rubber-stamped the document, and let my father through. The official could not know that such a name could never be bestowed, but only inherited. We were never real Kohanim, who are priests of the first tribe of Israel and very highly respected in all prayer assemblies.

My mother used the name 'Cohen' for a few years, then changed to 'Cowan' long before I was born. First of all, it was more Anglified, or should I say Scotified? And, secondly, there were so many people in the Gorbals called Cohen that it became extremely confusing. My sisters liked the anglicized version of Zeldon and often called themselves Seldon in making dates with new admirers.

Meanwhile, back in the kitchen, things were proving too quiet for us. We turned our attention to Kate, who adjusted her thick spectacles and turned over a fresh page of the weighty volume she was reading. We had only just learned a new jingle with which to tease her. 'Hey, Katie! Have you heard the latest?' She placed her finger on the page absent-mindedly and looked up. Jacky went on. 'You know. It's a new one about "Men don't make passes at girls who wear glasses".'

I added, 'He read it in an American magazine at the library.' My sister Kate shook her head. 'You kids! Starting again . . .' and went back to her book. She was learning not to react to our teasing.

She resembled my mother in one way. Once the vital personality shone through, you forgot that Kate ever wore glasses. And having more than her share of that unpredictable chemical called 'sex appeal' she had no fear of being left on the shelf of the marriage market. For more men made more passes at my sister Kate than at any other girl in our family. And that brought to me a new respect for the male mentality.

Looking up again, Kate said, 'Here, you kids! All of you!' She surveyed the kitchen. 'I'm waiting for my boyfriend. Try and look respectable like other families. And no remarks. Mind!' she threatened. Just then George came home, quite unusually early for him. Kate was on her way out with her intellectual-looking crewcut boyfriend.

George held his hands out to the kitchen fire. 'Pun my word! It's cold out there.' We all laughed. George carried an air of merriment with him. 'Is that a pun too, Georgie?' I enquired. He was a born funster, and in all his life he never could resist a game with a child. Lifting me up high, he hugged me as I dropped down. By magic, a piece of chocolate slipped out of his jacket sleeve, and he popped it into my mouth.

My brother George had been apprenticed to a furrier at age fourteen. And now he was twenty-one, Ma had scrimped and saved to open for him a small furrier's repair shop of his own. She never asked him if he liked the trade. There were no remarks passed in that connection. He knew the sacrifices that had been made for him. He was always playing around with words, making speeches, and explaining their meanings to us. He also wrote for the local *Jewish Echo* now and then. George had also written a play for our little Jewish dramatic group. His friend Avrom Greenbaum and he performed it in the Talmud Torah Hall.

Naturally, when George arrived in the kitchen, Ma turned to see him. 'What's the matter with you?' she said. 'Home early for a change?' Tall as Ma was, she still had to look up at him.

'Yep.' George ran his hand through his curly hair. He

104

pretended to act like a schoolmaster and pointed to Ma. 'You know what I saw coming down Main Street?'

'No, what?' we all replied. George laughed. 'You know those big metal cars that soldiers drive. Do *you* know, Ma?'

But Ma was busy back at the sink again peeling potatoes for the next day. 'Och, I dunno, leave me out of this nonsense.'

He turned to me. 'Well, Ebby. What are they called? Big metal cars that soldiers drive?'

'I know,' I said brightly. 'Tanks.'

'You're welcome.' He clicked his heels and bowed. 'Top of the class for you, miss.' We all applauded gleefully. Then George went on, 'And what are those big pieces of wool that Tilly is always knitting?'

'Hanks,' Jacky screamed. 'You're welcome,' George bowed again. 'And what is the name of the biggest toilet-pan makers in Scotland?'

'Shanks,' I laughed. 'You're welcome,' they all shouted.

Then one by one my sisters and brothers drifted off to bed. I was nearly always the last to go, and was certainly the last to get up in the morning. I lingered a while by the fire unnoticed. There was only Ma and George left in the kitchen. George's laughter-wrinkled face became serious. He edged over near the sink, where Ma was now peeling vegetables. She sensed he was near and turned round. 'Well?' Ma fixed her eyes on him. 'That's the earliest you been for years. What's the matter with you?'

'Ma . . .' George hesitated for quite a few minutes. Then went on. 'I'm engaged to be married.' She turned her back to him. Then she pretended to be busy at the sink. I guess she knew it had to come some day. But he was still her Sonny-Boy. He did not seem disturbed at her facing away from him. Maybe he was glad in a way.

'Ma.' George edged forward. 'That's not all. We're getting married soon and going to live in America. I'm closing up the business. It was never for me, that kind of work.'

I heard the clatter of her vegetable knife as it fell into the sink. She almost fell forward and gripped the window ledge over the sink.

'Ma!' he pleaded. 'Say something. For God's sake, say something!'

She kept her back to him. The clock ticked loudly on the mantelpiece. Standing very still, George waited and waited. He put out his hand. Then, without touching her, he drew back. Ma never turned round. At last George, too, went off to bed. After he had gone, I heard her racking sobs.

A BARMITZVAH

And two weeks later it was Saturday again. My mother, my sisters, and I were sitting up high in the balcony of the South Portland Street Synagogue looking down on George and Jacky. They looked like two young gods, adorned as they were in their white silk prayer-shawls with the crowns of their heads covered by little white satin yamelkies: Jacky, the Barmitzvah Boy, and George being given an honoured blessing on the Saturday before his marriage, a double ceremony quite unique in the annals of our synagogue. On this Sabbath morning, the Rabbi stood up high within the reader's desk in the centre of the synagogue facing the Ark.

Jacky, now thirteen, celebrating his barmitzvah, his coming of age in the eyes of all Jewry. They welcomed him as another man that the Jewish people could count on. Another man to make a minyan, a quorum to start the service. Another man to fight one day when we took Jerusalem. As it says in the final sentence of the Passover prayer-book, *'l'shono habo b'Yiroosholoyim* [and next year in Jerusalem]'. We did not know it then, but it was true in Jacky's case. For he did live to fight and dwell again in the Holy Land.

There had been a lot of happy talk about George's forthcoming marriage, but no further discussion about his departure for a new life in America. It became understood that his arrangements were proceeding quietly. My mother made it clear that she did not want to know his travelling date. We knew that Ma would not let George be married without bestowing upon him the honours which it befitted a Jewish mother to give.

So she arranged his oof-roof, his special bridegroom's ceremony, on the Saturday before his wedding, so that his marriage would be duly blessed. We were all there, dressed in our Sabbath best. The ladies and girls upstairs in the synagogue looking down on the panorama of numbers of men in their prayer shawls facing the ark. Then the ancient scrolls adorned in silver were brought forth.

George was first called and read a portion of the Law when the scrolls were unrolled before him. Then a few men of the immediate family were called up, one by one, to recite certain blessings as an honour. At last the Rabbi's voice rang out, calling Jacky's Hebrew name, 'Jacov Ben Zoosa Mordecai [Jacob, son of Simon]'.

Slowly Jacky walked forward from his seat in the congregation. Then, after hesitating for a moment, he climbed the few steps up to the prayer-desk. His tread became more firm, and at last he attained his position in front of the holy book. The Rabbi pointed to the Barmitzvah chapter, allocated according to the boy's birth date. Jacky cleared his throat. Then his boyish breaking voice echoed round the old temple in a haunting Hebrew recital from one of the five books handed down from the time of Moses.

He bowed and nodded at appropriate intervals. His sturdy figure, already manly, stood proudly erect. Jacky sang on, with only an occasional glance up at Ma above him in the balcony. I can only guess her thoughts. But I knew what long years of heartbreak and hard work it had taken to get them both to the bimah of the shul. There stood one of her sons entering manhood. His path, like the long carpet of the synagogue, stretching in front of him. And there was the other, eldest son, pushing his way out from under the warm blanket of his mother's love to try his strength in the world outside. I looked over at Ma. There was a tear trickling down her cheek. She gave a quick flick of her hand, so that no-one would notice the tear or the gesture. Perhaps she was thinking of the time when she ran miles to the hospital with George bleeding in her arms, his head split open by the railing in front of our tenement. Or was it about the time when Jacky lay all night dangerously ill with a fever?

We knew no doctor on whom we could call during the day, never mind in the middle of the night.

There must have been dozens of incidents running through her mind. But they all fade to nothing in the excitement of the great day in the synagogue. Happiness carries you forward and like an ointment soothes over all the hurts. My own thoughts were far away in the Skeoch woods. I could see the setting sun through the trees behind Jacky's half-naked body. Down there in the pulpit, he was not the boy that I knew. He seemed remote, like some handsome Egyptian prince. His puppy-fat had gone, and he had grown as tall and as broad as the promise of his boyhood figure.

I knew things would never be the same. He was a man and had stepped out of the smallness of our childhood games into his prematurely adult life.

So the ceremony ended. Our family and friends gathered in the vestry to drink a little wine and to greet us with many 'Mazeltovs' and good wishes again. We started off down the street homeward bound for lunch. Jacky walked with my mother's brother, Uncle Nathaniel Banks, who had turned up out of the blue. As we strolled down Apsley Place, I could clearly see the distinct line of the family resemblances. My mother's family, the Bankses, were nearly all tall, broad, and large of face and head. This strain followed through Tilly, George, Rina, and Jacky. Then my father's people were all smallish. Some were neat and petite like Rose, Rae, Kate, Annie, and Wally. Others were stocky like Lily and myself.

Uncle Banks was a fine figure of a man. He always reminded me of a picture I had seen of King Edward the Seventh. They might have been twins, dressed alike in the height of Victorian fashion.

Ma had other brothers and sisters who had gone from Lithuania to New York. Then on by covered waggon to Texas. But it was Uncle Nathaniel who met my mother when she, at the age of sixteen, landed at Greenock in the early 1900s. As soon as he met her, he explained about the kind of hard life to expect here, and added that she would have been better off to stay in the old country. Anyway, he for one, could not help her, and she would just have to look out for herself. So Ma found a room in the Gorbals and obtained work as a seamstress. Later she met Papa, and eventually they married.

Still, Uncle Nathaniel was a strange character. He was always drifting in and out of our lives. Sometimes he arrived immaculately dressed, even down to his gold watch and chain, loaded with presents for us. Other times he came hungry and unshaven to seek shelter. Ma bore him no grudge and always took him in, housed and fed him during his bad times.

We were walking towards home for our special Barmitzvah Shabbos dinner. A few of Ma's friends had gone ahead to collect the dinner-pots from Mrs Glick's oven, and were already setting up the tables when we arrived. Wally and I were relegated to the bedroom, as there was not enough space either in the kitchen or in the big room for all the visitors and reverend gentlemen. We passed the time unwrapping Jacky's presents, which were mainly fountain pens and religious books.

Wally and I lost no time in squirting ink all over the beds, over the chest of drawers, and over the books that Jacky would never read anyway. When the time came, Ma called us to the door of the big room. We edged our small heads round the door. Jacky was about to make his Barmitzvah speech.

Dinner was over. Everyone looked well-fed and contented, except Wally and me. The Rabbi paused in his address, ' . . . and I hope he will be a credit to the Jewish people and to his dear mother. And now I would like to call upon the Barmitzvah Boy to say a few words.'

We all clapped our hands and stamped our feet – shouting 'Speech! We want Jacky! Speak up, Jumbo-boy!' Actually we knew Jacky's speech better than he. For he had been rehearsing it in our bedroom for weeks beforehand. Jacky rose to his feet amidst resumed applause. And, as he spoke, I mouthed every word with him. 'My dear Mother, Reverend Gentlemen, Ladies and Gentlemen. Today I am a man.' There was prolonged applause at this traditional statement. Then Jacky went on: 'This is indeed a great day in my life, because I have today become a full-fledged member of the Jewish community. I fully realize that now I am barmitzvah, I am duty-bound to fulfil all the commandments of our faith. I can assure you, ladies and gentlemen, that I will endeavour to do so to the best of my ability. I must express my heartfelt thanks to my dear mother . . .' Jacky's voice choked a little, and he hesitated for a second, then went on, '. . . for all the love and care and attention she has lavished upon me. I can promise you, mother, that I shall try to be a source of joy and nachas to you. To the reverend gentlemen, I express my sincere thanks for their excellent tuition, and for making my barmitzvah celebration such an impressive occasion for me. In conclusion, ladies and gentlemen, I must thank you all for your lovely gifts, which I greatly appreciate. May we all meet again at many other happy seemchas!'

A great wave of applause and cheers flooded through the room as Jacky sat down. Wally and I were then called into the kitchen and served the remains of the feast for our dinner.

As I attacked an over-large helping of fruit pudding, the spoon stopped half way to my mouth. Quite suddenly, I felt sad. I knew that next year I would be sitting here alone. For then, Wally would have to go through *his* barmitzvah celebrations, synagogue, speech and all. He, too, would stand up and say, 'Today I am a man,' amidst rounds of applause. And I would be the only remaining child, officially, of our large family. The years were flying by. The boys could also leave the Hebrew school after they were thirteen. I would have to go there alone after school every day.

The next day seemed very quiet for a Sunday. For this was usually a busy cleaning day for my sisters. I dressed by the fire in preparation for my Sunday morning Hebrew school. The kitchen table was still cluttered with dishes. Really, it was not like Ma or the girls to leave it like that. Perhaps they had gone to return the tables and chairs borrowed for the barmitzvah. It looked as though there was no-one in the house but me.

George appeared at the kitchen door. He looked handsome in his best suit, dark coat, and bowler hat. 'Hello! Nobody at home?'

I finished dressing. 'It doesn't look like it,' I replied.

'Where is everybody?' he asked.

'I don't know. Where have you been?'

'Just out, my wee girl. Just out.' I looked up at him tearfully. 'It seems funny. Everything's so quiet.'

'I guess they must have found out.'

'Found out what, George?'

'Well,' he said slowly, putting his hat and coat over a chair. 'I suppose it's the best way really.'

'I don't know what you mean, Georgie.'

'I've been round the whole house. There's nobody here. Someone must have told them I was leaving today.'

'You mean, going away for ever?' I cried. 'But what about your wedding? And all the plans?'

'There were no real plans about the wedding. Your wee listening ears misled you, as usual.' He pulled my ear. 'I never intended to be married in Glasgow. We were getting a special licence in London and going off to the States. But I hadn't the heart to tell Ma the exact date.'

'But why did they leave me here all alone?' I sobbed.

'You know,' he wagged his finger at me. 'You were always the last to get up in the morning. Mind I used to tell you it'd get you into trouble one day?'

'But me!' I stood there crying like the child I was. 'The only one to say goodbye out of this big family. And you know how I hate goodbyes.'

'Well, then, let's not say them.' George put on his hat

112

and coat again. I made no move towards him. He did not approach me, but turned round with his hand on the kitchen door. 'So long, little Ebby. Keep well and take care of our Ma.'

I thought it was goodbye for ever. But years later my brother George returned to Britain and settled in the city of Newcastle in the north of England. He visited Ma and the family in Glasgow quite often. In Newcastle, he made a good name for himself as a member of the City Council there. And one day in the middle of a busy election campaign as a candidate for Member of Parliament for his district of Newcastle, he was taken ill. Two years later he died, after much suffering, of a brain tumour. On his death bed he looked like a man of eighty, yet he was only fifty-six years old. The only time I ever thanked God that my mother was dead was when I looked down upon my big brother George's gravestone.

On that day of his departure from Apsley Place, Ma returned about half an hour later and came into the kitchen.

'George has been here.' I tried to hide my tears. 'I know,' she replied. Then she started to clear the table of the dirty breakfast dishes.

'But, Ma! He came to say goodbye. He's going away to America.' I squeezed myself between my mother and the sink and gazed up at her.

'I know.' Her voice was dead flat.

'But didn't you want to see him for the last time?'

'I saw him,' Ma said quietly. 'I saw him from Mrs Schulberg's front window.'

Ma looked down at me. I could see her eyes were rubbed and bloodshot. 'He looked nice. Didn't he?' she said proudly. I nodded my agreement, at the same time swallowing the lump in my throat.

Then Ma turned me away from the sink towards the kitchen door.

'It's time for you to go to chader. You are the only Hebrew scholar left in this house.'

113

'But, Ma,' I pleaded. 'What about poor Georgie? There was no-one here to say goodbye.'

'I know.' She turned back to the cluttered kitchen and rolled up her sleeves. 'You are not the only one who does not like to say goodbye.'

A VERY HOLY NIGHT

And so we come to the end of September 1929. Rosh Hashannah, the Jewish New Year, was upon us once more. And eight days after that came Kol Nidrei night, the eve of the Day of Atonement, the holiest day in the Jewish calendar.

My mother had warned me to be in good time for the meal that night as she had to go to the synagogue early. And my heart pounded madly as I raced along Apsley Place in the Gorbals of Glasgow. I glanced over my shoulder. Yes, they were still after me. Small finger-shaped shadows pointed their accusations at me. On this holy night my sins were almost upon me. I must atone for my sins.

There was a weird atmosphere in the darkness of the silent street. The feeble gleam of the little gas mantles failed to light up the distance between one lamp-post and the next. Not a soul could be seen walking the pavements or crossing the road. For this was Kol Nidrei night, the eve of Yom Kippur, the holiest day of our year.

A musty tomb-like air hung over the tenements. I ran into my close. No protecting safety swept down to enfold me that night. As I trod fearfully up the stairs, I could almost see through every Jewish door. There stood the sinners, one and all, laying out their best clothes to go to the synagogue and pray for forgiveness.

The next day they would fast all day, without so much as a drop of water through their lips, so that all their transgressions of the past year should be wiped out. Then they could begin a new year with a clear conscience.

'Oh, God!' my little eight-year-old brain throbbed, as I jumped the stairs two at a time, 'forgive Mr Vineberg for short-weighting the meat.' I had heard Ma accusing him of this. And I prayed that Miss Duncan's own God would forgive her for hating children.

Ma was already dressed and ready for the evening service. My sisters were hurrying on with the dishwashing. A cold meal awaited me in the kitchen. It was to be my last food until breakfast the next morning. Children were supposed to fast for one evening. Adults fasted for twenty-four hours until the end of Yom Kippur was signalled by our Rabbi blowing the ancient Ram's Horn.

Rosh Hashannah, the Jewish New Year, had come and gone. It had been two glorious days of feasting and fun. Yet there were prayer services in the morning and in the evening. And in between we prayed, because we knew that in eight days time the Day of Atonement would be upon us.

Between the New Year and the holy fast-day, there had been a Sunday. Following tradition, we paid our yearly visit to the cemetery to say a prayer on our father's grave. The tiny headstone, shaped like an open book, bore the name 'Simon Cowan'. My mother, surrounded by the family, bent forward in grief. She knelt down and pulled at little blades of grass which protruded from the plain drab grave. There were no flowers, as our Jewish religion does not permit them.

My sisters and brothers held their prayer-books and, sobbing, read out the service for the graveside. I stood staring down at the small piece of white marble. Not one tear did I shed. I felt nothing. I could never believe that the body of a man really lay under that portion of brown earth. And even further beyond my belief was the fact that this man had been my father.

For our return from Riddrie cemetery to the Gorbals, we boarded the private bus which the congregation provided for their annual visitation. As I sat down, a wonderful feeling of survival surged through me. I was only eight years old. Death seemed far away. The reassuring presence of my mother and my family was all around me.

I felt the warm blood of young life seeping through my

veins. As the bus turned the corner of the cemetery road, I peered through the back window. Hundreds of white head stones merged one into the other. They did not frighten me. I reached into Ma's shopping bag, searched out a sandwich, and munched it as we journeyed home.

These were my thoughts as I sat in the kitchen, on the eve of the Holy Day of Atonement, eating the last supper. Ma lifted my final plate from the table. 'I'm going to shul now,' said Ma, hurriedly serving the quick meal. She already had on her hat and best black coat. 'Mind, now! Not a drop of water do you take until tomorrow,' she threatened me as she prepared to leave. 'Tomorrow,' she said, 'I will fast all day and ask God's help for another year. Even a child like you can fast for a few hours. You got plenty to think about.'

My assenting eyes agreed with her. There was a scramble as the rest of the family grabbed their coats and followed her. The Kol Nidrei night service was so solemn that children were not usually taken. I was all alone in the house. Two tall white candles burned high on the kitchen table, which was covered by a white cloth. The candles were the only lighting in the whole flat. Ma had turned off all the gas so that she would not need to touch a light when she returned. The family had to undress in the darkness of their bedrooms and grope their way to bed.

I moved over and sat beside the dying fire. My small figure huddled down on the stool against the comforting warm black grate. Gazing upwards, I felt God was near me. He appeared to be staring at me from the corner just where the glare of the fire ended at the ceiling. He looked kind. Ma had always said He was kind. God had been good to us, she would say, providing food the day that she was left a widow with eleven children. He had looked after us in our need.

I was not afraid of Him. I knew vaguely that there were other Gods that other people believed in. I had listened to the forbidden Christian prayers every morning in school.

'Give us this day our daily bread. And forgive us our debts as we forgive our debtors.' I repeated snatches of the morning prayer.

Their father, Jesus Christ, did not seem much different from my own Jewish God, who was the only father figure I knew. But at the age of eight I was afraid to mention this to my mother. All over the kitchen walls my sins were written, in shadows, haunting me. I thought of the many lies I had told Ma during the year gone by. I would speak silently about this in the synagogue tomorrow, hoping for forgiveness. Then I shook my head in regret at the thought of the forged note to the teacher after I had stolen half a day from school.

Suddenly I remembered my greatest sin of all. I had eaten a forbidden slice of buttered bread, given to me by my gentile schoolfriend Jean, on a Passover day. Oh! that lovely moment of succulent abandon, like all such moments, soon to be paid for in a Hell of remorse! The clock ticked like a metronome in my head. There was a creaking noise from the dark pit of the lobby. I feared man not God. Nothing on earth would have moved me from the protecting candle-light. I listened carefully. The hall became silent again.

I peered up at the clock. But in the dim light I could not make out the time. It seemed like days had passed since my last meal. But it could not have been more than three hours. What a long evening! I ran my tongue over my cracked hungry lips. My throat was dry and parched. 'Water?' I cried to myself. If only I could have a drink of water! Now I knew why the soldiers of the Foreign Legion staggered in agony across the desert.

Once more I heard a noise. Though it had been there all the time. It was the constant drip of the tap over the sink. Here was a way out of my painful thirst: I edged over towards the sound. Sharp, cutting pointers of candle-light flickered over me. I bent over the sink. What a relief it would be to catch just one drop of water on my tongue. In the full knowledge of my guilty desire I glanced round. It was now or never before the family returned.

I thought I heard voices on the stairs. In a matter of minutes they would all be home again. There could be no rescue from my fort of thirst until the next morning. As I leaned over the sink, my tongue hanging out for succour, the moon came out from behind a stack of chimneys on top of the flour mills. It lit up the window, catching my reflection on the pane. I really saw myself that night. I was a small fat female creature, soft in body and in mind. Only a few short hours ago I had acknowledged God's goodness. I had thanked Him for his kindness to my mother and my family when they were poor and hungry.

Now this snivelling, perpetual sinner, this me, unwilling to endure an hour or even a moment of self-denial. I saw myself as the weak-willed female being that I would surely grow up to be. I drew my tongue back. Then my body slumped to the floor, sobbing. On her return my mother carried me, stirring in my sleep, from under the kitchen sink into the warmth of her bed.

A FANCY-DRESS PARTY

Stubborn shreds of snow had newly melted from the pavement cracks in our street. Yet the early spring of 1930 had not unfurled enough courage to appear, when Purim, a happy festival, came upon us. This festival, at the tail-end of winter, celebrated one of the finest victories that we Jews achieved in Biblical times. The victory was over Haman, the Hitler of olden days.

According to our Bible story, after the death of Solomon, the tribes split. Ten tribes broke away and formed Israel. The other two tribes however, stayed loyal to Solomon's son. When the Persians conquered Israel, they took the ten tribes to Persia.

Many years later Ahasuerus ruled Persia, and he chose Esther as his wife. At that time the Prime Minister was Haman, an Amalekite. Haman ordained that everyone should bow down to him but Mordecai, Queen Esther's uncle, refused to do so. Therefore Haman hated the Jews. He tricked the King into giving an order for the Jews to be destroyed. At the risk of her life, Queen Esther confessed she was a Jewess. The King, as he could not take back his command, supplied the Jews with weapons. Then a war followed in which the Hebrews were victorious.

Modern Jewish people still remember Haman because he tried to destroy us. And thousands of years later in our family kitchen in a high tenement in the south side of Glasgow, my mother shaped a thick dough into facsimiles of small three-cornered hats. She filled them with sweetened poppy-seed and raisins and baked them in the oven. They were a delicacy which once tasted were never forgotten. We could buy them in the Jewish shops in the Gorbals or snatch them hot from our mother's apron. So we ate our 'haman-tash', our reproduction of Haman's hat, to celebrate the fact that he was hanged on the gallows he had erected for Mordecai the Jew.

It was a happy time for the inhabitants of the Gorbals of 1930. There were flags and banners and fancy-dress parties. The Megillah, or story, was read out to all the children at our special Purim service in the synagogue. Whenever Mordecai's name was mentioned we clapped our hands and cheered. Then each time we heard the name Haman, we whirled our wooden rattles noisily, booed and hissed, and stamped our feet to show our disapproval of our old enemy.

Year after year, at the community's annual fancy-dress party, the small girls of the neighbourhood came dressed as Queen Esther, in their veils and long dresses, their heads adorned in crowns of silver paper. The boys, with home-made swords, were either Mordecai or Ahasuerus, or just common soldiers of the tribes.

According to the gossips in Apsley Place, that year was to be no different. The communal party was free, which was fortunate for me, as my mother still could not afford too many luxuries. And certainly her budget did not stretch to all the sandwiches, cakes, and lemonade which my insatiable female nine-year-old appetite devoured.

I usually attended the party uniformed as a foot soldier in cardboard armour. But that unforgettable year, much to my own sorrow, I decided to break with tradition. It was the eve of Purim. The fancy-dress parade was soon to begin in the synagogue hall. My two brothers and I were at home in the kitchen. On the bare floor, my brother Jacky was kneeling down cutting out cardboard armour for Wally's soldier costume.

I could never get used to the Jumbo-boy looking so grown up in his long-trousered suit. But he was still young enough to want to be in on the Purim fun. Jacky pushed me off the important piece of cardboard upon which I had been

121

standing. Wally stood nearby, dangerously whittling away at his rough wooden sword.

'This uniform should have been ready.' Jacky waved the scissors at me irritably. 'It's only a few hours to go.' Then he straightened up and looked at me. 'Hey! Shouldn't I be cutting two of these outfits? One for you?'

'No.' I stubbed my toe against the kitchen table leg. 'I'm not going as one of your old soldiers. I'm fed up with them.' Jacky threw his head back and laughed. 'OK. Be fed up. So you'll finish up as Queen Esther with one of Ma's old lace dresses.'

I threw a lump of sugar at him. 'No. I won't. I won't. You know I'm not the Queen Esther sweety-faced kind.'

'You're right.' He looked me over in his frank brotherly way. 'You've got a face like a pudding and a pair of shoulders like a centre forward.'

'More like a goalkeeper with pads inside,' murmured Wally.

I looked for something else to throw. 'Flattery will get you nowhere.'

Jacky rose to defend himself with his cardboard shield. Wally hurriedly gathered up his wooden shavings. 'All right.' They both backed against the kitchen sink. 'So what will you do?' enquired Jacky. 'You haven't much time.'

'Don't worry about me,' I shrieked, near to tears. 'I've got my costume all ready. And I'm going to get dressed now.'

'What is it?' the boys asked in unison. 'Come on, tell us. You never said.'

I hesitated for a moment. Then blurted, 'I'm going as Charlie Chaplin.'

The two boys looked at each other in astonishment. 'But Charlie Chaplin has nothing to do with the festival of Purim,' said Jacky.

'I know.' I stamped my feet in girlish anger at him. 'But there's no rules about the fancy-dress parade. Betcha I win a prize!'

'Your bet's on.' They both laughed.

I could hear their laughter as I ran through the lobby into our bedroom. I pulled out my costume, which was in an old box under the wardrobe. Then I laid the whole outfit, lovingly, on the bed. In secret, I had been gathering it for months. There was a cast-off pair of Jacky's long trousers, ripped and tattered. A dark grey tail-coat left by some uncle from a wedding. Big brother George's old bowler hat, moth-holed like a colander. And lying nearby, a pair of battered muddy football boots. Also a tin of black shoe polish for my eyebrows and moustache.

Dressed and on the way out, I lifted Ma's shabby black umbrella from the coat-stand in the hall. In the gay Purim streets of the old Gorbals, nobody seemed to notice a little female tramp aged nine. My coat-tails blowing in the icy breeze, and almost losing my big boots, I clattered along Apsley Place up to the Talmud Torah Hall in Elgin Street.

Proud mothers and pretty children were arriving for the fancy-dress party. I had not dared let my mother see my costume. I was afraid I would not be allowed to go. I slunk in with a crowd of boys dressed as soldiers. They did not seem to be amused by my outlandish figure.

Large groups of merry fancy-dressed children danced all around me. Their costumes were carefully made and looked expensive. There were dozens of Queen Esthers and scores of Mordecais and Amalekites brandishing swords. But the only small forlorn raggedy Charlie Chaplin was me.

I edged over towards the stage at the end of the hall. A stout member of the Ladies' Guild handed me a numbered ticket. 'I suppose you want to enter the competition?' She grinned down at me over her fat chins. 'Yes, please.' I pushed up my big bowler hat, which was not only encompassing my head but almost my small shoulders too. 'And please,' I pleaded, 'after the judging, could you mark down that I'm going to sing a song? There's an extra prize for that.'

'Certainly.' Her bosom was shaking with concealed laughter. 'You *are* bold! There's not many kids going for two prizes.'

'Well, I've seen some of the prizes over there,' I confided to her. 'And I do fancy that fishing-rod for my brothers. Although they don't always take me with them when they go.'

My motives were not entirely altruistic. I reckoned the boys might accept the rod as a bribe to take me along when they went fishing. Fixing on my huge cardboard placard, she said, 'I hope you'll be a big success.'

'Thank you.' I nearly nodded off my hat again.

Some official blew a whistle as a signal for the fancy-dress competitors to assemble. The audience sat in chairs gathered round the walls. Then the children went round in a circle in the centre of the floor. Two ladies and two men, prominent in the community, were the judges.

We circled endlessly around. I could hear titters of laughter as I passed my fair-weather friends of Apsley Place. My two big brothers pretended they did not even know me. As I clumped around the giggling circle of children, I had great regrets. Shaking my head sadly, I wondered what made me think of such a stupid outfit for a Purim party.

At last the prizewinning number was called out. It was not mine. I might have known. The winner was Ida Tenter, the only child of the well-to-do family down the street. She did look beautiful, as Queen Esther, with her long dark ringlets. I had always admired her in all the lovely dresses her mother had made for her, while I played alongside in my sisters' hand-me-downs.

When they handed Ida the prize, a little tear trickled down my cheek and made my boot polish moustache start running. I smudged it with my outsize jacket sleeve. Then suddenly I shook myself out of my gloom. All was not lost. There was still a prize for a song or a poem by someone in an original costume.

The audience quickly drew their chairs along in rows and

faced the stage. My spirits were rising now. Hitching up my trousers, which were forever slipping down, I ran round to the back of the stage. I was just in time to wait my turn. A big lumpy boy was on stage singing, 'I belong to Glasgow.'

The song brought the house down and everyone joined him in the chorus. This took a long time. I was panic-stricken. Then a charming little girl, dressed as a fairy, danced a short ballet piece.

'You're on now, dear. Good luck!' The Guild Lady gave me a push.

I found myself in the centre of a stage for the first and only time in my life. The lights dazzled me. My heart was sinking rapidly. But I gathered my small courage, twirled my tattered umbrella and clumped forward, almost tripping over the untidy laces of my big football boots.

Jeers and hisses were coming from the back rows. But the adults soon quietened them down with 'Give her a chance! Be fair, now! Give the wee girl a chance!'

I cleared my throat and heard a strange plaintive voice which I realized was my own. It wavered:

> *Oh! The sun shines bright on Charlie Chaplin*
> *His knees are knocking . . .*

I wobbled my own knees through my baggy trousers.

> *His boots need blacking.*
> *Oh! The sun shines bright on Charlie Chaplin,*
> *Before they send him to the Dardanelles!*

Repeating this, the only verse I knew, my pathetic little voice trailed off. I stepped back, swept off my dusty bowler hat and bowed. Then I marched off in raggedy dignity.

We were then called back on stage. There were only three prizes for such a large number of entrants. And I got the third prize. Still, it ended in a very happy evening for me, because when the guild lady showed me the remaining choice of prizes, the fishing rod had not been claimed.

Through the cold gas-lit streets I ran happily homeward bound. Warming me were visions of my brothers and myself fishing off the pier-end at Rothesay in the summer.

THURSDAY WAS
BLACK-WATER BATHNIGHT

And the next day was Thursday – black-water bathnight.
My brothers Jacky and Walter were four and three years
older than me. We three had one bath every week in the
water from which our teenage sisters, Rina and Annie, had
just emerged.

The kitchen fire heated a water-tank at the back of its
range. Coal was comparatively cheap in Scotland in 1930, but
my mother had a tight budget and every atom of economy was
important. Hot water had to be used to the best advantage.
So one bath full of water served five or more children.

My sisters had a young friend Mabel, a pretty, waif-like,
motherless girl, who frequented our home. My mother often
served meals to Mabel and popped her into the bath, sometimes unaware that she was not one of the family.

Thursday was also a tedious night for my older sisters.
They were compelled to stay at home and polish the brass
candlesticks and all other brass ornaments, scrub floors,
and clean the house for the weekend. This led to innumer-
able fights, quarrels, and a general air of Thursday night
irritability. Only my married sister Rae enjoyed those evenings, because Thursday in Glasgow was the barbers' official
half-holiday. Rae and her husband Louis travelled on the
red tramcar from their flat in Shawlands for their weekly
visit home.

After tea Louis, tall and handsome as ever, assembled the
younger children in our family, placed a cushion high on a
chair, and proceeded to cut each child's hair. As soon as
we were shorn, Rae ushered us into the bathroom where
the steaming, but slightly used, water awaited us. First the
two girls, and sometimes Mabel, then my brothers and me.

Our home did not boast such luxuries as bath-towels. Ma always used clean but cast-off white bed-sheets to wrap us in.

Cold and draughty as the bathroom was, my sister Rae, dark, vivacious, and fun-loving as always, made an entertainment out of bath night, as she did out of everything. And while the older girls ran to the kitchen fire to rub themselves down, Rae scrubbed and shampooed us younger children. Then she grabbed one child, concealed from head to toe in a white sheet, and ran through the draughty lobby calling, 'Who's coming?' Rae laughed as she ran. 'Who's coming . . . ?' Everyone by the fireside had to guess which child Rae had in her arms.

Ma gave the white bundle a prod. 'H'm . . . I tink it's Jacky. It's too big for Evelyn.' After much giggling I would throw off the makeshift robe and reveal my clean nude body. Ma looked me over while her outstretched hand warmed my vest by the fire. 'Oh, my!' said Ma, pulling down her glasses to examine me better. 'Oh, my! You did get big since last Thursday. I tot it was one of the boys.'

Rae cleaned my ears with the screwed-up corners of the sheet, rubbed me down and helped me on with my fresh underwear. But on that Thursday night, my mother looked anxious despite the gaiety of the warm kitchen. For my sister Rina, then aged seventeen, had not arrived home from her day's business in Dunoon. She had not had either her supper or her bath.

Being grown-up, for some time, Rina had often rebelled against this communal bathing. But I knew, as did the rest of the children, that this was not the reason for her absence. My sister Rae looked up as she dried my hair with a small cloth. She had noticed Ma's worried look.

'What's the matter, Ma?' Rae enquired.

'Rina never came home yet,' mumbled Ma. 'I'm terrible worried. It's been a stormy day. Do you think something is wrong with the boats on the river?'

'Now, don't worry.' Rae laughed off this thought. 'She'll be OK. There's not been a steamer sunk on the Clyde between Dunoon and Gourock in a hundred years. You know fine and well where Rina will be.'

'Maybe you're right,' Ma shrugged. 'Still, it's a worry.'

'Do you want me to go out and look for her, Shveeger?' Louis enquired of his mother-in-law.

'No. No.' Rae threw him a warning glance. Then Rae's face became serious as she looked at Ma. 'I can't understand you, Ma,' said Rae. 'Really I can't. I never understood why you kept Rina back from that boy all these years.'

My mother, developing into one of her stubborn moods again, did not answer. Rae went on, 'I think you won't admit you were wrong. And it's a darn shame. A young couple like that. Hounded from pillar to post. Not allowed into his parents' home and not welcomed here. Courting in back closes like that. It's mad!'

Ma never replied. We children kept unusually quiet by the fire. My sister Rae seized her opportunity on Rina's behalf, and kept talking. 'He's a nice boy, and they make a fine couple.'

'I got nuttin against him,' said Ma at last. 'He seems a good boy from a nice Jewish family.'

'So what's it all about?' Rae snapped.

'She's too young to settle down,' Ma said thoughtfully. 'She never seen the world. Going about with the same boy since schooldays.'

'Och, rubbish!' Rae retorted. 'She could do a lot worse.'

'So?' Ma snapped back. 'You don't know what you say. It's not good to be married too young. Soon you have lots of children. Worries and work. Worries and work.' Ma shook her head sadly.

Rae looked at her quietly. 'I never heard you talk like this before, Ma.'

'No?' replied Ma angrily. 'Well, I don't talk much. Who will I talk to?' Ma never waited for an answer when she was angry. 'It's all children here. I got no husband to talk things over with.'

Ma thought for a moment, then went on, 'Anyway, it's not for me that I'm saying all this. It's for Rina's sake. It's for all my daughters I'm thinking these things.'

Rae threw back her dark head and laughed. 'That's a laugh. And you a Yiddisher mama. I never heard of one of those keeping their daughters back from marriage.'

Rae glanced over at us bunch of kids huddling by the fire, and shook her head at Ma. 'You of all people, Ma. You wouldn't like to be a lady of leisure without your children.'

Ma pushed a strand of hair out of her eyes, almost knocking off her spectacles. 'Ach,' she shrugged. 'Doant take no notice of me. It's just these Thursday nights. The thought of all the weekend cooking and work.' My mother rested her hands on my young shoulders. 'God willing, I'll see my job through until the last one is married.' Ma shook her finger at Rae in pretended anger. 'Anyway, I got this family this far from hunger. And I don't need advice from you, Mrs Rae!'

My sister Rae realized she had gone far enough. But she could not resist driving home the last shaft of words.

'Well, I think it's daft,' said Rae. 'Rina and her boy are head over heels in love. And it's time they had everyone's blessing.'

We heard the front door bang in the hall, and through the entrance to the kitchen came our radiant Rina. She was all aglow, looking sweetly beautiful. The combination of her pink cupid's mouth, moist and young, and her shining golden wavy hair would have melted anyone but my irate mother.

'Where you been?' Ma wasted no time on greetings. 'You know I been worried about you. Can't you come home and help tidy the house for Shabbos instead of running around the streets with boys?'

I cannot remember any other time when the feelings of the occupants of our kitchen – Rae, Louis, Annie, schoolfriend

Mabel, Jacky, Walter, and myself – rebelled so much against my mother.

My sister Rina was not perturbed. Her love and happiness clothed her in a sort of immunity to the barbs of the world. 'That's not fair, to say that,' Rina pouted. 'You know I don't run around the streets. And I've never been out with more than one boy in my whole life.'

'Maybe that's true,' Ma said grudgingly. 'But you shouldn worry me. I tot something happened to you on the boat from Dunoon.'

'No. I'm all right. And I'm sorry if you were worried,' Rina apologized. Then she went on, 'As a matter of fact, I finished work early, and I've been into town a message.'

'What message?' Ma shouted. 'Who sent you a message before you get a hot dinner from a day's work?'

'Please don't get excited, Ma,' Rina begged. 'I've done nothing wrong.'

Slowly Rina drew her glove off her left hand and displayed the three-stone ring on her third finger. 'That's where I've been. I've got myself engaged.' Rina spoke haltingly, afraid of Ma's reactions.

Ma looked at Rina's hand, dumbfounded. We children nudged each other and started giggling. Rae and Louis stepped nearer to Rina as though to protect her. It was touch-and-go for a moment. Then Ma relented. I think my sister Rae's words had left their mark on my mother. Ma stepped forward, held Rina at arm's length almost tearfully. 'So that's it, then. Engaged? Eh?' She cleared her throat. 'Well, I wish you mazeltov and all the luck in the world.'

They clung to each other for a moment. Then all the family and Mabel gathered, kissed Rina, shook her hand at the same time admiring her ring and screamed, 'Mazeltov!'

'Well, Ma,' Rina smiled happily. 'Can I bring my fiancé round tonight? We're officially engaged now.'

'Aa right,' answered Ma. 'If you like. Bring him round. I

never had anything against him. He seems a nice Yiddisher boy.'

'He's the best,' murmured Rina dreamily. 'Maybe we won't have much money to begin with,' Rina went on, 'but we'll always have each other.' And they did, too.

All this time, Rae's husband Louis had been spectating quietly at our family scene. Now he came forward and stood beside his wife.

'Maybe now's the time to tell the Shveeger our news.' He looked at Rae. 'Plenty of time for that,' Rae tried to stop him. But my mother could be sharp of hearing when she wanted to be. 'Now, what's the matter?' she said apprehensively. 'Well,' Louis grinned sheepishly, 'we're going to have a baby.'

Immediately Ma went over to my sister Rae, guided her into a straight-backed chair and laid her arms outstretched on the kitchen table. 'My goodness! Don't move,' cried Ma. 'You should've told me. Somebody else could have bathed those kids tonight.'

Louis beamed from one big ear to the other. 'Och, don't fuss,' Rae smiled. 'I've never felt better in my life. Anyway, is that all you have to say to me, Ma? Don't I get a mazeltov?'

Ma smiled back. 'I'm pleased. But you don't get no mazeltovs until I see a nice fat healthy baby, please God.'

'What would you like us to have, Shveeger?' Louis grinned. 'Me?' shrugged Ma. 'I don't mind. Boys or girls. I got all sorts of children. Like dolly mixtures. A mixed bag. What do you want yourself?'

Rae interrupted. 'He wants a girl, of course. He always wanted a daughter.'

'That's right,' Louis winked. 'First a girl, and then a boy.' This came true. But at that moment Rae smiled. 'One at a time will be enough, thank you,' she said, looking at her husband.

Over by the kitchen fire, Annie, Mabel, the boys, and me were fidgeting and pretending not to be listening too hard.

But at last I could contain myself no longer. The whole evening, with its excitement and revelations, had made me quite emotional, as usual.

I rushed up to Rae and threw my childish arms around her. 'Oh, Rae,' I cried, 'I heard about the baby. You'll be busy with it. Who's going to bath me on Thursday nights? You'll be in your own house, and I'll miss you.'

My sister Rae lifted me on to her lap despite her husband's protests. 'Don't you worry. I've already thought of that. You'll come to my house. You and me will bath the baby, and then I'll bath you. Then Louis will bring you home. How about that for a date?'

I gave her a big hug. 'I'll poke your baby's ears the way you do it to me.'

'Oh, you wouldn't hurt my baby! Now would you?' Rae said knowingly. 'No, no,' I laughed. 'I'll love it to bits for ever.'

The kitchen was bouncing with joy as we talked about this new double event in our family. With the corner of her apron, Ma wiped a tear from her eyes. 'My, it's not been like my usual Thursday night at all. Such a lot of tings happening.'

Suddenly my sisters' friend, the emaciated Mabel, stepped forward. 'I'll need to go now, Mrs Cowan. My dad will be worried about me.'

'Oh, Mabel!' Ma gave her a gentle push. 'I forgot all about you in the excitement. Will you be all right going home?'

'Yes, thanks,' shouted Mabel on her way out. 'And thank you for letting me have the bath.'

My mother stood between her two happy daughters, then addressed herself to Rina.

'Well,' said Ma, 'at least your share of the bathwater wasn't wasted. Mabel had a bath.'

MY MOTHER'S BIRTHDAY

And the following Thursday was my mother's birthday. She never knew the exact date of her birthday. All she remembered was that it came in May every year during Shavuos, the Feast of Weeks, which commemorates an historical event – the lawgiving on Mount Sinai. It was also a harvest festival.

I knew that Ma had a harvest of small gifts awaiting her birthday. My sisters and brothers had been saving up for some time. But they had money to spend. All the other older members of the family were working. Even the two boys, Jacky and Wally, nearest to me in age, were delivering milk and newspapers. So they had a sixpence or two to spare.

My pocket money was one halfpenny per week. And if my mother received a gift of a box of chocolates, I was given one chocolate instead of my precious weekly ha'penny. This set my plans back a little.

Nevertheless, by dint of saving, scraping, and scrounging liquorice sticks and other sweet things from my friends at school, I had saved my weekly ha'penny for twelve weeks and now had a sixpence saved to buy my mother a birthday present.

Now that money was no longer the real problem, the hardest choice seemed to be what one small girl could give to the woman who had almost nothing. I did not know where to begin. Even a minute necessity was a luxury to Ma.

All the same, I earnestly intended to have something ready when the others handed over their gifts. So on the day of my mother's birthday I threw my satchel into the lobby, ran away down Apsley Place, turned right and over the forbidden tram lines into Crown Street, Glasgow South.

There, along the busy thoroughfare, sprawled a panorama

of sweetie-shops, hardware and chandler stores, grocers, butchers, and green-lit chemists' shops. Tightly clutching the precious sixpence in my inky school-sticky hand, I set out on my first solo shopping expedition. In the chemist's window, I could see exotic perfumes with prices to match. In the confectionery shops the cheapest box of sweets, with a fancy wrapping, cost at least a shilling.

Feeling dejected, I shuffled on until I stopped at a little cut-price hardware store. Buckets and basins, shovels and spades were strung outside. Hanging over the narrow entrance were doormats, cards of doorknobs, hammers, and chisels. It had started to rain. I edged in from the wet pavement to the shelter of the overhanging pails. Then I ran my eyes round the crammed shop window.

There were small copper vases, china dogs and jugs, combs, brushes, and notebooks in imitation leather cases. Suddenly my eyes focused back on something they had passed over. There it was! The present I wanted for Ma.

Tucked in the corner, near the back window, I could see a pair of silverized round combs, such as a lady would wear when drawing her hair up for an evening out. I pressed my chubby nose against the rain-splattered window and gained a closer look.

I knew I would not visit another shop that day. The combs were the gift I wanted for my mother. Just then I caught sight of the pencilled ticket. My heart sank. The ticket read: 'Useful Gift. One shilling per pair.'

This was a setback I had not anticipated. For I had made up my mind to look at things which cost only sixpence. Filled with stubborn hope, I resolved to go inside and see if I could by some chance negotiate with the shopkeeper. I shook the raindrops from my dank urchin-like hair as I ambled over to the counter. A dishevelled little man came shuffling out from the kitchen at the back of the shop.

As he leaned towards me, I could smell his extremely bad teeth, which together with his tobacco-filled breath nearly knocked me over. 'And what can I do for you?' he wheezed. I tried what I supposed was the nonchalant approach of the very rich who are not interested in prices.

'I'd like to see that pair of silver combs at the back of the window, please,' I replied.

'Oh! Yes.' He made towards the window. 'Fancy yourself as a great lady, do you?'

'No. No. They're not for me,' I exclaimed. 'They're for my mother's birthday.' He returned with the card of combs in his hand. 'Well, you've got great ideas. They'll be the very thing for your mother to wear when she's dining out,' he said sarcastically.

Perhaps he guessed from my appearance that Ma was grateful that we had enough to eat when dining in, never mind out. I fingered the tiny silver dots on the comb. 'They're really lovely. Just what I want.' I tried hard to appear detached, but my anxiety showed. 'But they're much too dear. One shilling a pair!' I shook my head. 'Much too dear.' The untidy little man was certainly more discerning than I imagined. 'How much have you to spend?' he enquired. I knew the game was up. 'I've only got a sixpence,' I grinned.

'H'm.' His dirty fingernails made a scraping noise against his unshaven chin. 'What can we do about that, I wonder?' Furtively, he glanced around the shop. It was a quiet mid-week afternoon. His busy days were Friday and Saturday. 'Tell you what, lassie,' he leered. 'Come into the back shop with me and we'll talk things over.'

My thoughts were too involved with my own urgent problems or I would have realized his intentions. For I had heard my sisters speak often of men like that. And my strict instructions were to run for my life on such occasions. 'What do you mean?' My innocent nine-year-old eyes held his. 'Nothing,' he pleaded. 'Honest! I mean it. Nothing. I won't do you any harm. Just come in to the back and we'll have a wee kiss. And then I'll give you the combs for sixpence.'

I knew I was doing wrong and that the whole situation spelled danger. But I had to have the gift for my mother that afternoon. My sisters and brothers had arranged to hand Ma her birthday presents at the supper table. Soon the shops would be closing. For the first time in my young life, I suffered the blindness of desperation.

'OK. But mind, now . . .' I warned him in childish naïveté. '. . . Just one kiss. Nothing more.'

The man lifted the flap at one end of the counter to allow me through. My heart throbbed like the engine of a Clyde ferry boat. I could hear his floppy slippers shuffling behind me as we entered the back shop. Turning round to face him, I pressed my back against the sink. He came towards me. The stench from his bad breath made me want to vomit.

The little man leaned down, and as he forced his rough lips to mine, he placed his hands upon my breasts and pressed hard. After a minute of this smelly torment, I pushed him aside and whispered hoarsely, 'That's enough, now! You promised.'

'Aye, ye're right.' He was not the least bit excited. 'Ye're right.' He shook his head sadly. 'It is enough. Though if I'd been twenty years younger, your wee present would have been quite different.'

Stepping back, he turned away from me. I saw my chance to escape and pushed the sixpence, which I had been clutching moistly all this time, into his hand. On the way out of the shop, I grabbed the card of silver combs still unwrapped.

Feeling deeply ashamed and physically sick, I raced back to my own neighbourhood. As I turned the corner of Apsley Place, I almost ran into the back of my sister Kate returning from work. 'Hey!' she said, turning, and grabbed my panting young body. 'What's up?'

'Oh, Katie, it's you! I'm so glad. I'm in terrible trouble.'

My sister Kate was the one I turned to in all my troubles. She was my guide, my second parent. Kate was full of concern. 'Why? What's the matter?'

'Oh, Kitty, help me! I'm going to have a baby.'

A faint smile turned up the corners of her mouth. But she still looked worried. 'You're mad. That's not possible.' Then she realized that under her hand, which was resting on my small shoulder, stood a trembling frightened child. My sister Kate was a well-balanced, bespectacled, intelligent girl in her teens. It must have been obvious to her that in reality something was terribly amiss. She put her arms round me now and drew me into our closemouth. 'Now, look here,' she said, shaking me gently. 'Let's start at the beginning. Nice and calm, now.'

I was far from calm. 'I told you. I'm going to have a baby,' I sobbed.

'But that's not possible. You're far too young.' I glared up at her. 'I'm not. I am a girl. Aren't I?'

'Yes. But you're still too young,' Kate replied. 'You don't understand about these things.' She appeared more worried now that the conversation began to penetrate her mind. 'Now, come on. I can see you're upset. And if something has happened, we'll go to the police and get a doctor, too, for that matter.'

At the mention of so much authority, great sobs ran through me. 'Oh! No, please! They'll put me away. I'm a bad girl.'

Gently, Kate forced me against the wall of the close, and ran her eyes over me. My clothing was not too disarranged. 'Come on, now,' she said firmly. 'For the last time, I warn you. Tell me exactly what happened. Right from the beginning.'

Glancing round to make sure nobody was about, I whispered. 'It was the man. The man in the wee hardware shop. I went in to get a present for Ma, and he kissed me on the mouth.' I gasped excitedly. 'And now the seed is sown and I'm going to have a baby. I can feel it inside me already.'

'My God!' Kate gasped in alarm. 'What else did he do? Besides kiss you?'

138

'He squeezed my breast,' I cried. My sister Kate's face was a study in expressions. She was angry, anxious and half laughing at the same time. 'But you haven't got a breast. You're only nine years old.' She smiled faintly. Then she looked serious again. 'Did he do anything else?' She stepped back and looked afraid. 'For God's sake! Did he touch you anywhere else?'

'Well, no,' I choked, then went on. 'He kissed me. His big dirty lips touched mine. Then he put his hands on my bosom.'

'And anywhere else?'

'No, honestly, Katie. Then I gave him the money and ran like the hammers.'

'You're sure, now . . . Sure?' she said strictly.

'God's honour.' I lifted my childish hand to heaven. 'I grabbed the present and scooted for my life.'

I produced the card of combs in a gesture of triumph. I was feeling a bit better now. 'Look, Katie. I got it for Ma. Her birthday present. It's real nice, isn't it?'

'Yes, it is.' She scarcely glanced at the gift. 'But I tell you what,' Kate said thoughtfully. 'Don't mention this to Ma. It would spoil her birthday. There's no harm done, luckily. All the same, tomorrow I'll report that horrible man to the police.'

I shook my head vigorously. 'Oh! no, please!'

'They won't bother you,' said Kate. 'And a man like that should be reported. It's a blessing there was no real harm done.'

My sister Kate's steady eyes held mine. 'Now, you must promise me faithfully that you'll never do such a thing again.'

'Chadi shem.' I mouthed a Yiddisher oath.

With a sigh of relief Kate wiped her spectacles, which were steaming by now. Then she took my hand, and together we started up the stairs to our home.

After we had climbed halfway, I tugged at her hand and made her stop. She looked down at me.

139

'You're sure about the baby?' I begged of her.

'If you told me the truth.' She emphasized the last word. 'I am sure. And when you're older, I'll explain it all to you.'

Katie squeezed my hand and walking close together, my head hardly touching her waist, we entered our flat on the third landing. My sisters and brothers were all gathered round the kitchen table. Ma was sitting in her usual place at the top of the table, not dressed special at all, and almost unaware that it was her birthday. Kate and I were late, and from their angry looks, I gathered we had kept the family waiting.

As soon as my sister and I assumed our places at the table, each member of the family rose in his turn and handed Ma their gift. There was no cake, no candles or singing. The little bare ceremony was most embarrassing, for we were not a family given to sentimentality.

The older members of the family walked up, pushed their little parcels in front of Ma, muttering, 'This is for your birthday, you know.'

Ma was more abashed than any of us. She lifted the packages, opened them in silence, held the gift up in admiration and said, 'It's very nice. Real nice. Tank you.'

Being the youngest, I was always the last for everything. But my turn finally came. Katie gave me a push. I tumbled over the chair-legs and up to my mother's place at the table. I handed her the card of combs, still unwrapped. 'This is for you. Happy birthday,' I mumbled.

Ma smiled down at me and lifted the combs to inspect them more closely. 'Oh, my!' Her voice wavered a little. 'They are lovely. Jus' like real silver. I'll wear them one day.' Ma patted the top of my drooping head. 'Tank you,' she said. Then she looked round the table, cleared her throat, and said, 'Tanks. All of you.'

Quickly she lowered her head over the cups, lifted the teapot, and started to pour out the tea. I was still standing near her, feeling a bit disappointed. My great sacrifices not sufficiently praised. Ma noticed me and looked round. I hesitated

'Did you really like the present, Ma?' I jerked out my words. 'You know, the combs.'

Ma set the teapot down and casually handed me a cup of tea, saying, 'Of course. I said tanks, didn't I?' Then she suddenly realized that I was waiting for something more. She picked up the combs from where they were lying on the table. 'My,' she said, 'they must have been very expensive!'

My sister Kate had come up behind me. She looked down at me and smiled. 'Yes, they were.' Wide-eyed and innocent, I grinned back at her.

The memory of my horrible experience with the man in the shop was melting rapidly in the warm presence of my childhood idol, my sister Kate, and the subdued happiness of my mother on her birthday.

THE LAST FRIDAY NIGHT

The years flew by – Passover, June, July, Rothesay, the Island of Dreams, Rosh Hashannah, the Jewish New Year, the Day of Atonement, Chanukah at Christmastime, our Scottish New Year's Eve, Purim in the spring, Ma's birthday in Shavuos in May again. And at last we came to a Friday evening in May 1932.

Every Friday night, on the eve of the Sabbath, my mother lit her Shabbos candles. First she fixed them into brass candlesticks, newly polished by my sisters. Then she stood them on an old brass tray and placed the tray in the centre of the kitchen table, which was covered by a fresh bleached-white cloth.

Then my mother covered her head with a small lace handkerchief, as a mark of respect for the Sabbath candles. She spread out her work-worn hands to the puttering flames of the candles and, being unable to read either Hebrew or English, Ma said in her own brand of Yiddish: 'Thank you, God, for another good week. And, God . . . bless this house and all the people in it, and make them good boys and girls until next Friday night . . . Amen'.

The family were gathered round the table, the boys with their caps on, the girls' heads bowed. We all echoed, 'Amen.' My mother then lifted a little bottle of her home-made wine, poured a small quantity into a wine glass, and handed it to my brother Jacky. He stepped forward, holding the Siddur, with his finger marking the page, and sang from the prayer book, in perfect Hebrew, the Kiddush for Friday night.

At the end of the Kiddush, Jacky sipped from the wine glass, handed the glass to Ma, who in her turn took a quick sip. After which the glass was passed round to every person at the table, each swallowing a sip.

'Good Shabbos,' one said to the other as the wine was passed along. Finally, Ma placed the bottle of wine in the cupboard until the next Friday. There was only one difference on this Sabbath eve. It was the last Kiddush we would celebrate in our home in the Gorbals. For the removal to our new home, in the suburbs of Glasgow, was to take place in the following week.

Ma and the family sat down and our Shabbos supper of gefilte and chopped fried fish, bread, butter, and tea was served. The real Shabbos dinner would, of course, be served on Saturday at lunchtime. When the Friday evening meal had been eaten, and after their usual quarrelling, the girls started to clear the table and wash up the supper dishes. From high up on the mantelpiece, Ma lifted my brother George's letter from America. Ma had learned to distinguish between the President on the American stamp and the King's portrait on the British mail. She had treasured her son's letter all day.

Ma settled down by the fire. The glow from the brightly burning coal and the flicker of the Shabbos candles made an unforgettable picture round our family hearth. When the kitchen had quietened a little, Ma said, handing me the letter, 'Now. Read me Zeendle-Sonny's letter.' Glad to be excused from my share in the washing-up, I proudly read out loud in my best schoolgirl letter-reading voice:

May, 1932

Dear Ma and all,

I hope this finds you all in good health, as it leaves Doris and I here in Los Angeles. Things are very tough here at the moment, what with the depression having caused great unemployment, poverty and consequently crime. But I don't say all this to worry you, because I'm writing to let you know that at last I have found a good job. It is with an insurance company. And as I have to go round the branches collecting money, they gave me a gun and I

143

carry it all the time. Jacky and Wally will be interested in this . . . .

They were. The boys were listening in muted excitement, while Ma covered her mouth with her hand to stop herself from crying out. I continued with the letter:

Anyway, although they have taught me how to use it and I have fired it in a practice range, I have not used the gun officially yet.

It is all very strange here. The people are not so friendly as in dear old Glasgow.

I miss you all very much.

Ma! try and get somebody to write me a letter, please! Big hugs and kisses all round and a special kiss for the boys and wee sister Ebby.

Ever your loving son,

George.

My mother slipped the letter from my hand and looked over the handwriting as though she could read. 'My goodness! A gun!' she exclaimed. 'It's so dangerous. I hope he'll be all right.'

'Don't worry, Ma,' shouted Jacky, his mind already fired with George's adventures. 'That guy can take care of himself.'

Suddenly Jacky pointed his forefinger at Wally as though he were firing a gun. '*Rat-a-tat-tat*,' Jacky's voice imitated gun-fire. 'And another redskin bit the dust.'

'*Rat-a-tat-tat*,' Wally quickly replied, pointing his gun-finger in return. 'And another sheriff turned in his badge.'

The two boys fell to the floor clutching their stomachs as though mortally wounded. Not to be left out, I threw myself on top of them. Soon we were a shrieking mass of squirming arms and legs.

'Ach, stop that!' Ma pulled Jacky's shoulder. 'Is there no peace in this house even on a Friday night?'

We broke up the fracas and moved into a corner of the kitchen. The evening had settled down. Some of my sisters had wandered down to the flats below to visit friends. Katie sat reading a book by candlelight. Ma dozed off in the old nursing chair by the fire, still gripping her Sonny's letter.

The clock ticked into a dull time for Jacky, Wally, and me. We had to stay dressed in our best clothes. We were not allowed to play out in the street on the Sabbath eve. Neither were we permitted to write games or cut puzzles with scissors, so as not to desecrate the Sabbath.

The boys and I retreated to their bedroom. This was not exclusively their room, for it was shared by our teenage sisters Rina and Annie, who slept in a double bed next to the boys. I slept in my mother's room, sharing a bed with my sister Kate. But my brothers' room was the place where we played on rainy days and Friday evenings. We were bored and looking for mischief. George's letter had obviously made an impression on Jacky.

'Oh, boy!' shouted Jacky, jumping from one bed to another. 'That's for me! America, the wide world, and lots and lots of guns.'

'You wouldn't like it,' I answered thoughtfully. 'George is very homesick. You can tell by the letter.'

'That's a lot of hooey,' retorted Jacky. 'I don't believe it. Homesick! There's no such thing.' He threw a pillow at me. In its flight it burst open, filling the room with feathers. I jumped about trying to catch a feather in my hand. 'He is. He *is* homesick! And anyway,' I puffed, 'you're not going anywhere. I won't let you go.'

'Oh-ho,' Jacky leered, pointing his gun-finger again. 'Try and stop me, ma'am,' he said in his best American movie accent. Wally came towards me, blowing feathers from his mouth. He put his arm around me and said in his quiet way, 'He's kidding you on. He's too young to go away, anyway.'

Jacky had become very belligerent now. 'I won't always be young. You'll see. I'll be off as soon as I'm old enough.'

The Jumbo-boy jumped down from the bed he had been bouncing upon and faced me. 'And I won't write you any of those sapsy letters. Dear old Glasgow, and all that rot! I'll be too excited, out in the world, to care about you and your old Glasgow.'

He thumped his broad chest. 'You'll never be a big shot like me. You're always clinging to your ma.'

Tears were in my eyes now. 'Well, I like Glasgow,' I bubbled. 'And I'm always going to live here. And I'm not going to let you go.' I was sobbing now. 'I'm not going to let any of you go. Not anybody in this whole family.'

I threw the leaking pillow back at him. We could hardly breathe in the atmosphere of flying feathers. Jacky was in his boyishly sadistic mood. 'Och, rubbish!' he shouted. 'We're nearly all gone already. George is far away. The four sisters are married. Rina's engaged. We're all going and gone.' He hammered his fist down on the old chest of drawers like an auctioneer. 'Going, going, gone!'

'He's just teasing you.' Wally threw a comic book at Jacky.

'I'm not.' Jacky ducked and pushed his face near to mine. 'She knows it's true.'

'It's not,' I cried. 'I'm going to keep what's left of us, right here. Right here in Apsley Place.'

'And how will you do that?' Jacky's large figure loomed over me. I thought quickly. 'I'll build a big gate. Just like in the Queen's Park . . . Yes,' I went on expanding this idea, 'a big gate with huge spiked railings. And I'll keep the keys and I'll never let you go. You'll see.'

'Where did you get that story from?' asked Wally, clearing himself a place on the bed beside me.

'I dreamed it. I dreamed it the other night.'

'You did not,' threatened Jacky. 'It's one of your stories again. Out of your head.'

'It's not,' I cried. 'It was a real dream.'

'There's no such thing as a real dream.' Wally shook his head at me. 'It's you and your imagination again.'

146

I leaped up, turned down the gas mantle and the bedroom was hushed and dark. Standing on the bed, I waved my arms in a ghostly manner. The shadows of our three youthful figures stretched against the walls.

'No,' I whispered, carried away with the spirit of my words. 'No. It was a real dream. There was this big park. Inside it, I hammered and I banged the spiked railings and then built the gates. And I was the keeper. Only little old me had the keys. And because I was in charge, not one person got away. Nobody. Not Ma, not the girls, nobody. I kept them all locked together for ever.'

The bedroom creaked darkly for a moment.

'Sounds spooky,' said Wally, glancing furtively over his shoulder.

'No. It's not.' My small hand groped for his to reassure him in the darkness, as I still try to do to this day. Then I went on, 'Because in the middle of the park, stood our home with all the family inside it.' My voice turned into a singing tone. 'And up the stairs on the third landing,' I went on, 'inside the house, everything was light and warm and happy. Nobody gone. Nobody married. Just Ma and the family living happily ever after.'

There were a few moments of silence, then Jacky said hoarsely, 'That's a dream, for sure, Ev. You'll never keep us locked together for ever.'

'But you'll get hurt, out there,' I cried. Jacky turned up the gas light, rubbed his eyes and blinked over at me. His aggressive mood had vanished, and the real Jacky returned. 'There's nothing you can do about that.' His sensitive eyes recognized my sadness. 'Here we are on the move already. This our last Friday night in the Gorbals. We'll never see Apsley Place again.'

'And who wants to?' retorted Wally in his unsentimental way. 'Just wee Bubbly-Face over there.'

Wally pointed to my weeping figure on the bed. 'She's got the waterworks behind her eyes turned on again.'

'Leave her alone,' said Jacky. It was his turn to protect me. 'Come on now,' Jacky gave me a shove. 'Get to your own room. We'll tidy up here. What a mess! Ma will be angry. You know she won't clean up on Shabbos.'

'OK.' I wandered across the hall to my bedroom. As I turned, I could see, through my tear-blurred eyes, Jacky's broad figure outlined against the doorway. I wiped my eyes with the back of my hand.

'Don't forget to wake me. I want to go to the synagogue tomorrow.' I sniffed. 'Please don't leave me behind.'

Jacky ran his hand through his fair hair and adjusted the newly acquired grown-up braces on his trousers.

'I'll try not to,' he said quietly.

Safe in my own bed that night, I listened to the familiar night noises of our home. I could hear the bleep of the broken cistern in the bathroom. Then the creak of the boys' bed as they turned restlessly in their sleep.

Across the room, in the corner where George's bed once stood, a shaft of moonlight fell on the empty space. In the bed next to mine, Ma lay snoring gently, her tired, weary body resting for a few precious hours.

I lay back to back with my sister Kate, and close as we were, she never heard the sound of me . . . a child crying in the night.

GOODBYE TO THE
VANISHING GORBALS

And so Monday came, and with it the big removal van. In huge white letters painted across the side of the black removal van ran the words:

WE MOVE YOU ANYWHERE.

It was a warm sunny day in May 1932, yet darkness filled my eyes. My heart sank lower with every piece of familiar furniture carried out of the closemouth. Anywhere? Where was Anywhere?

I just knew it would be a miserable place with well-lit closes, trim back yards and strangers with whom I would not care to play out in the street. At last it was goodbye to my dream of childhood in the Gorbals of Glasgow. But which is the dream and which the reality? Did that street ever exist? Or is it only a comforting corner of a child's grown-up heart, as every Apsley Place must live in your heart and mine?

Yes, we lived in a street – an ordinary place – of garbage smells, ringing bells, and neighbours' quarrels. No real street could fulfil the dream of memories all gone, of people long dead. Lily, Ma, George . . . Oh! Ma, where are you? If I did believe that their spirit lives on, where else would I seek them but in this crumbling neighbourhood now vanishing from an age long gone?

'Cooooo-eeeee! O-O-O-oh-p-e-n! Who's coming?'

The Angel of Death did not always pass over our home. He visited us. Yet the spirit of my mother's Chanukah lights and the fun of Purim lives on in my children.

'We move you Anywhere.' Anywhere! 'There is nowhere,'

I cried to myself. Ma's decision to move out of the Gorbals had not been sudden. The idea came slowly, from my sisters' social aspirations, like the constant drip of water wearing away a stone. I can still hear my sister Kate's voice: 'But, Ma,' she protested, over and over again. 'Everyone's moving out of the Gorbals. Just everyone. What kind of an address is Apsley Place to give to my friends?'

'I dunno,' Ma replied. 'There's nuttin wrong with it. It's a goot house here. Anyting of this size in another distric would be too dear a rent for me.'

'But we don't need a big house any more.' Kate went on. 'Rina's getting married. There's only five of us left. I'm in the business. The boys are working. We can all help with the rent.'

When the factor's annual missive came in April, we had until the first of May to decide about the house for another year. Kate brought the matter to a head.

She came striding into the kitchen one day, adjusted her spectacles and said determinedly, 'Look, Ma. I want you to come out and see this flat in Shawlands. It's just the place I've been looking for. It's two rooms and kitchen with a little scullery.'

'And about the rent?' Ma glared at her.

'The rent is not any dearer than it is here.' Kate added, 'Of course, it's a much smaller flat altogether. But the district's very exclusive.' Then Kate played her trump card.

'Just think, Ma, a little scullery where you could close the door on the cooking and make the kitchen like a living-room. No food smells.'

Our numbers at meals were becoming smaller. At that moment there were only my mother, Kate and myself sitting round the kitchen table.

'It sounds too posh,' I interrupted. 'And what about school? I can't leave now just before my qualifying exam for senior school.'

Kate dismissed me with an airy wave of her hand. 'Och,

you'll be all right. Children of your age adjust themselves very quickly.'

'That's what you think,' I shouted back at her. 'But I'm not leaving Abbotsford Primary until I get into senior secondary school.' Although we were always chipping at each other, my sister Kate and I had this tremendous rapport between us.

'Tell you what, Ev.' Kate had an instinct for applied psychology. 'If Ma likes the new flat, I'll pay your tram fare back to Abbotsford School every day until you pass your qualifying exam. Then you can chose a school near here.'

So off went Ma and Katie with a card to view in salubrious Shawlands, the Jewish working girl's Shangri-La. I heard later that Ma quite liked the district. She was so fond of flowers, and there was a lovely oblong garden running right down the centre of the street. Ma had her doubts about the scullery. It was no bigger than a cupboard, she told me, with a gas cooker and a sink. You could not turn round in it, but would have to back out holding a pot. Still it meant that you could eat in a living-room, not a kitchen, and this was a big step up in the world.

No direct mention was made of the fact that bed-settees were to be opened each evening in the living-room and front lounge (if you'll pardon me) . . . as there was only one small bedroom. My sister Kate prevailed on Ma. And as there was not too much expense involved, my mother agreed to the move.

Looking back on that scene, on a May day in 1932, I can see my short schoolgirl legs dangling over the back ledge of the removal van. I watched an old bed being bashed into the van: the bed which once slept Annie and Rina giggling away into the night, its headboard scratched with the heart-shaped names of their sometime sweethearts.

Then came the battered chest of drawers with the marks of our inky escapade at Jacky's barmitzvah party. There wobbled the old mangle, its rollers worn thin from countless washdays. Piece by piece our household was lifted down by

151

the dark overalled men. To me, they were like pall-bearers at a funeral.

At last Ma came out of the close loaded down, as usual, with shopping-bags, from the corners of which hung old soup ladles, odd carving-knives, and a big black kettle. I know not what her thoughts were as she departed from our home of many years, or whether she had shed any tears before descending. But without once looking back she climbed up beside the driver. The rest of the family were at work and were to meet us in our new home.

One of the mover's men gently lifted me into the van. 'Come on, lass. Back you go. You'll fall off that edge. What are ye starin at, anyway?'

Leaning out, I still looked backwards, and I always will, as they fastened up the drop half-door. Goodbye to my best friend Rosie Schulberg! Goodbye snottie Natie Hornstein! Goodbye to our big kitchen table from which so many eager young faces had already departed! Goodbye for ever to the makeshift Passover grocery store, and the fading ghetto life of Glasgow Jewry! And so I waved a last goodbye to the vanishing streets of the old Gorbals.

As the van rode on its way, grimy tenements disappeared. Neat red sandstone buildings replaced them. Shawled and aproned little housewives were left behind. And walking round the shops, I could see ladies in smart coats wearing fashionable hats.

Young as I was, I could feel the wind of change. For Shawlands was only a few miles and three short decades away from our brave new world of two-car garages and keeping up with the Cohens out in the Mearns.

It was late afternoon as we drove into Bellwood Street. The street was wide and clean. Colourful flowers were in bloom in the gardens down the middle of the sunny avenue. Some children were playing out after school. At the windows, edges of lace curtains moved slightly as Ma trudged up the few steps to the tiled close.

I skipped along beside her. A short marble flight led up to our new home. In contrast to our previous flat, we only had one neighbour opposite us on the brief landing. Turning left into the front door of the new flat, I found myself in a tiny square which, for sure, was a hall not a lobby. There would be no room for Ma's stands of plant pots here.

There were two doors to the right and two doors to the left. Four people could be crushed to death trying to pass each other.

The sweating, puffing removal men were working hard, angling furniture in. Most of our larger pieces had been sold before the flitting. I walked into the living-room and shivered. There was no homely black grate, just a neat modern interior fireplace in which lay some dead ashes. Everything looked bare, bleak, and small. Opening a door I peeped into the much-desired scullery. Compared to it, the black hole of Calcutta would have been Paradise.

I hopped around trying to avoid the mover's men. 'Ach you,' shouted Ma. 'You're right under my feet here. Can't you go out to play?'

'I've had a look out in the street, Ma.' I shrank against the door. 'The kids are awfully well-dressed, and they look like terrible snobs.'

Ma threw me a quick searching glance. 'The children will be easier than the grown-ups. Don't worry. Off you go.'

'But, Ma,' I cried. 'I'm shy. I can't face them.'

'Maybe they're more shy than you. Shy people are often mistaken for snobs. You'll be aa right.'

So I brushed my hair, donned my best gym tunic and went out to play in the street. Over by the electric lamp standard (the first one I had ever seen) were some boys and girls. I ambled across and leaned on a railing near them. They were playing cricket (ye gods!) against a white chalk-marked wall. Since I was the newcomer, and they did not appear to notice me, I thought I had better make the first move. 'Hullo there,' I said. Their communal 'Hullo' sounded pleasant enough. Then the smaller of the boys came forward.

'Care for a game of cricket?' he enquired.

'No, thanks,' I replied hurriedly. 'Football's my game. Anyway, it seems a bit light to be playing out. What about the cops?'

The boy shrugged. 'Cops! Never see a policeman about here.'

'Gosh! You're lucky. I could tell you some stories about cops.'

The rest of them gathered round and I regaled them with tales (mostly imaginary) of cops in the Gorbals. My adventurous past appeared to go down well. At last one boy said, 'My name's Peter Reilly. And this is my sister Emily.'

'How do you do?' Emily simpered. She sounded as if she had a permanent caramel toffee in her mouth. Peter jerked his thumb over his shoulder. 'That brute over there is Andrew MacIntosh.'

'Pleased to meet you all.' I tried to round out my words. Andrew MacIntosh came nearer. He was an extremely well built lad of thirteen or so. I had already noticed him. As he turned towards me, the sun caught his blond hair, his blue eyes, and a light auburnish down on his cheeks.

For a moment there seemed to be no-one else in the street except him and me. 'I heard your stories,' he laughed. 'You've had an interesting life.'

'Yes. If you live long enough and survive the cops and the dykes.' I tried to be sophisticated and smiled up at him.

'How old are you, anyway?' he enquired.

'Eleven,' I replied.

I ran my eyes over his gold-edged blazer and striped tie. 'What school is that?'

'The Academy,' he said quietly.

'H'mph! I always had a secret ambition to meet one of those saints.'

'You're a scream.' He threw his head back and laughed.

154

'Football and cops, and all. You're not the least bit like the girls around here.'

He did not speak for a minute or two. Then he stubbed his toe against the pavement and said, almost inaudibly, 'You can call me Drew. I don't let everyone call me that.'

'It's a nice name.' I was flattered but could not think of a better answer. There was a pause. Drew did not look up from his toe-stubbing activity. 'Know why this place is called Bellwood Street?' he enquired.

'No. Why?'

He spoke quietly, almost muttering. I leaned forward to hear what he was saying. 'There's a bluebell wood at the end of the street. Maybe we could go there some time and grab some bluebells after school.'

I shook my head. 'No. Don't fancy that.' But I thought to my tomboy self, first cricket, then flower-picking. What next? Drew looked up. At last his eyes met mine. 'I see,' he grinned engagingly. 'But there's something else you don't know.'

'What's that?' I asked.

'Near the end of the wood, there's an old deserted convent. A ruin. The ghosts of tortured nuns are supposed to haunt the place.'

I sprang to life. A haunted nunnery with ghosts! The future seemed full of promise. If we got lost, Drew could be big brother and bring me home.

'That's the best news I've heard all day. Do you mean it? Haunted?'

'Yes, honest.' He stood firm. 'I'll take you there. Tomorrow if you like.' I nodded vigorously.

'OK, then,' he shouted as he made off. 'See you tomorrow after school.'

I reeled dreamily into the sun-splattered close. It felt good to be alive. What a lovely street to live in! A haunted convent and a handsome boy called Drew who vaguely resembled my brother Jacky. I mused up the stairs . . . Mrs Andrew

MacIntosh. It sounded nice. Up to now my fancy of married names ran to dark sallow boys called Schuster or Shafar. But Mrs Andrew MacIntosh, that was really high class.

I waltzed up the short flight to the first landing. This building was beautiful, well lit, and yet secluded. It had a dignity not to be found in dirty old tenements. I turned into our new house. A cheery carpet had been laid in the hall. The fire now burned brightly in the living-room. Ma had done wonders with the smaller remains of our large furniture.

A clean starched cloth adorned the table set for tea. I popped my head round the door of the scullery. Appetizing smells wafted from the little place. It did not seem so small after all. I had not noticed the cheery little window.

There stood Ma, her hair almost as white as her apron, her tallish figure bending over the new gas cooker. I looked around the cosy room. There was still a lot to be done. But it was home. Ma turned her head from above the frying-pan.

'Noo? How did you get on?'

'Fine, Ma. They're nice kids. There's a boy . . .' I blushed and my voice trailed off. Ma had her back to me again and I was glad she could not see my pink face. Whether she heard my last words or not, I don't know. But she gave me a minute, then turned and waved her fish-frying knife at me.

'You see. I tol' you. You shouldn't have such quick ideas again.' She resumed frying. 'Nearly all God's people are good. You get the bad one now and then. Just like in a bag of potatoes. So you soon get rid of them. But give the others a chance, and don't judge so smartly next time.'

I nodded in youthful agreement, the words scarcely sinking in. But I remembered them often in later years and tried hard to apply my mother's simple philosophy as I licked my worldly wounds.

After Ma's little homily was over, I skipped across the hall and through a door facing me. This front room, which my sisters insisted on calling the 'lounge' was to me just the big front room. In it there was a large bay window, bright and alive with sunshine, facing on to the street.

I looked around for Ma's familiar landmarks. Not one living plant could I see. Then into my mind penetrated the thing which my conscious mind had ignored on my first glance round.

I looked again. Oh! Mother, no! How could you? For there on a window table, high enough for all the new neighbours to see, was a vase of artificial flowers.

**THE HOUSE BY THE DVINA
A RUSSIAN CHILDHOOD**
by Eugenie Fraser

'Eugenie Fraser has a wondrous tale to tell, and she tells it very well. There is no other autobiography quite like it'
Molly Tibbs, *The Contemporary Review*

A unique and moving account of life in Russia before, during and immediately after the Revolution. *The House by the Dvina* is a fascinating story of two families, separated in culture and geography, but bound together by a Russian-Scottish marriage. It includes episodes as romantic and dramatic as any in fiction: the purchase by the author's greatgrandfather of a peasant girl with whom he had fallen in love; the desperate journey by sledge in the depths of winter made by her grandmother to intercede with Tsar Aleksandr II for her husband; the extraordinary courtship of her parents; and her Scottish granny being caught up in the abortive revolution of 1905.

Eugenie Fraser herself was brought up in Russia but was taken on visits to Scotland. She marvellously evokes the reactions of a child to two totally different environments, sets of customs and family backgrounds. The characters on both sides are beautifully drawn and splendidly memorable.

With the events of 1914 to 1920 – the war with Germany, the Revolution, the murder of the Tsar, the withdrawal of the Allied Intervention in the north – came the disintegration of the country and of family life. The stark realities of hunger, deprivation and fear are sharply contrasted with the day-to-day experiences, joys, frustrations and adventures of childhood. The reader shares the family's suspense and concern about the fates of its members and relives with Eugenie her final escape to Scotland
'A Wholly Delightful Account'
Elizabeth Sutherland, *The Scots Magazine*

0 552 12833 3

THE PAST IS MYSELF
by Christabel Bielenberg

'It would be difficult to overpraise this book. Mrs Bielenberg's experience was unique and her honesty, intelligence and compassion makes her account of it moving beyond words'
The Economist

Christabel Bielenberg, a niece of Lord Northcliffe, married a German lawyer in 1934. She lived through the war in Germany, as a German citizen, under the horrors of Nazi rule and Allied bombings. *The Past is Myself* is her story of that experience, an unforgettable portrait of an evil time.

'This autobiography is of exceptional distinction and importance. It deserves recognition as a magnificent contribution to international understanding and as a document of how the human spirit can triumph in the midst of evil and persecution'
The Economist

'Marvellously written'
The Observer

'Nothing but superlatives will do for this book. It tells its story magnificently and every page of its story is worth telling'
Irish Press

'Intensely moving'
Yorkshire Evening News

0 552 99065 5

A SELECTION OF BIOGRAPHIES AND AUTOBIOGRAPHIES AVAILABLE FROM CORGI BOOKS

☐	99065 5	**The Past is Myself**	*Christabel Belenberg*	£3.95
☐	13588 7	**Daughter of Shanghai**	*Tsai Chin*	£3.99
☐	13126 1	**Catherine Cookson Country**	*Catherine Cookson*	£5.95
☐	13582 8	**The God Squad**	*Paddy Doyle*	£3.99
☐	13070 2	**Born Lucky: An Autobiography**	*John Francome*	£2.95
☐	12833 3	**The House by the Dvina**	*Eugenie Fraser*	£4.99
☐	99347 6	**A Time to Dance, No Time to Weep**	*Rumer Godden*	£4.99
☐	13586 0	**Susan's Story**	*Susan Hampshire*	£2.99
☐	12863 5	**The Long Journey Home**	*Flora Leipman*	£3.95
☐	13550 X	**Diana's Story**	*Flora Leipman*	£3.50
☐	13374 4	**House of Tomorrow**	*Claire Lorrimer*	£3.95
☐	99336 0	**To Be Young**	*Mary Lutyens*	£3.50
☐	99333 6	**No Going Back to Moldova**	*Anna Robertson*	£3.99
☐	12072 3	**Kitchen in the Hills**	*Elizabeth West*	£2.50
☐	11707 2	**Garden in the Hills**	*Elizabeth West*	£2.50
☐	10907 X	**Hovel in the Hills**	*Elizabeth West*	£2.99
☐	13347 7	**Insufferable Little Children**	*Elizabeth West*	£2.99